THE AMISTAD REVOLT AND THE TRANSATLANTIC SLAVE TRADE

PEOPLE and EVENTS That CHANGED the WORLD

THE AMISTAD REVOLT AND THE TRANSATLANTIC SLAVE TRADE

Richard Worth

Enslow Publishing
101 W. 23rd Street
Suite 240
New York, NY 10011
USA
enslow.com

Published in 2016 by Enslow Publishing, LLC
101 W. 23rd Street, Suite 240, New York, NY 10011

Library of Congress Cataloging-in-Publication Data
Worth, Richard.
The Amistad Revolt and the Transatlantic Slave Trade / Richard Worth.
pages cm — (People and Events that Changed the World)
Includes bibliographical references and index.
Summary: "Describes the revolt of the Amistad and the affect it had on the slave trade"— Provided by publisher.
ISBN 978-0-7660-7378-4
1. Slave insurrections—United States—Juvenile literature. 2. Amistad (Schooner)—Juvenile literature. 3. Antislavery movements—United States—Juvenile literature. I. Title.
E447.W665 2016
326'.80973—dc23
2015025536

Printed in the United States of America

To Our Readers: We have done our best to make sure all website addresses in this book were active and appropriate when we went to press. However, the author and the publisher have no control over and assume no liability for the material available on those websites or on any websites they may link to. Any comments or suggestions can be sent by e-mail to customerservice@enslow.com.

Portions of this book originally appeared in the book *Cinqué of the Amistad and the Slave Trade in World History.*

Photo Credits: Throughout book (textures): Eduard SV/Shutterstock.com; cover, pp. 1, 6 © Randy Duchaine/Alamy; New Haven Colony Historical Society and Adams National Historic Site/Wikimedia Commons/La Amistad (ship).jpg/public domain (ship on spine); p. 9, Interim Archives/Archive Photos/Getty Images; p. 11 Rischgitz/Hulton Archive/Getty Images; p. 14 Nathaniel Jocelyn/Wikimedia Commons/Sengebe Pieh (Joseph Cinqué)/public domain; p. 17 MPI/Archive Photos/Getty Images; pp. 18, 85 Library of Congress, Prints and Photographs Division; pp. 22, 32, 36, 46, 74, 95, 113 © North Wind Picture Archives; p. 24 Marzolino/Shutterstock.com; pp. 26, 29, 39, 48, 63, 66, 69, 71, 76, 80, 98, 109 Everett Historical/Shutterstock.com; p. 43 Georgios Kollidas/Shutterstock.com; p. 52 Hulton Archive/Getty Images; p. 56 Universal Images Group/Getty Images; p. 60 Hugh Manatee/Wikimedia Commons/View of New London, Connecticut, from the Shore Road.jpg/public domain; p. 82 Hulton Archive/Archive Photos/Getty Images; p. 87 Wikimedia Commons/GovRogerBaldwin.jpg/public domain; p. 90 Wikimedia Commons/Schooner Grampus.jpg/public domain; p. 101 Wikimedia Commons/Henry D. Gilpin, Attorney General of the United States (trimmed). jpg/public domain; p. 107 Ragesoss/Wikimedia Commons/Austin F. Williams Carriagehouse and House, August 31, 2008.jpg/CC BY-SA; p. 116 STR/AFP/Getty Images.

CONTENTS

CHAPTER 1

Revolt at Sea!

For Joseph Cinqué, a twenty-five-year-old rice farmer in Sierra Leone, Africa, it was the day that changed his life. In 1839, while walking peacefully along a dirt road outside his village in Mende, he was ambushed by slave traders and clapped in chains. Then Cinqué was taken on a journey to the west coast of Africa, where he found himself thrust roughly into a barracoon, or slave barracks. Many other Africans—men, women, and children—were also being kept there. They had been roughly seized and taken from their homes on a long, frightening journey that would finally end in the New World, and a life of slavery.

Each of these people had become the prisoner of Don Pedro Blanco, the wealthiest slave trader in the district. Don Pedro, "a combination of European gentleman and African king," represented a powerful slave trading organization based in Havana, Cuba.[1] He lived in great luxury at the mouth of the Gallinas River on the African coast. As historian Daniel Mannix explained:

> Don Pedro kept a stock of more than a thousand slaves in ten or a dozen barracoons on a series of marshy islands. On another island near the mouth of the Gallinas, he had his business headquarters, run by a general manager with the assistance of two cashiers, five bookkeepers, and ten clerks . . . On still another island was a sort of palace, where he lived in barbaric splendor with only his sister for company, and on still another was his harem. . . .[2]

Slaves were brought to Don Pedro's enormous compound at Lomboko after being captured by African tribes. There, they waited for a ship that would carry them on the long journey to plantations in the Americas.

A Long Sea Journey

Along with five hundred other Africans, Cinqué was led on board a Portuguese ship named the *Tecora* to begin a journey that would take approximately two months. The men were chained together and spent most of the voyage below deck, cramped into an area barely four feet high. They could not even stand up. The women and children were confined separately.

During the period of the Atlantic slave trade, historians estimate that as many as 10 to 20 million Africans were forced to make a similar journey.[3] One man, named Olaudah Equiano, described the terrible experience this way:

A group of captive Africans is led to the coast, where ships will transport them across the Atlantic Ocean to a life of slavery.

> The closeness of the place, and the heat of the climate, added to the number in the ship, which was so crowded that each had scarcely room to turn himself, almost suffocated us . . . the air soon became unfit for respiration, from a variety of loathsome smells, and brought on a sickness among the slaves, of which many died. . . .[4]

As the *Tecora* approached the Spanish-owned island of Cuba, the conditions of the African captives improved. Because they would need to appear healthy to fetch a good price in the Havana slave markets, Cinqué and the others were brought up on deck for longer periods. Here, they were unchained, dressed in clean clothes, and given better food to eat. Instead of sailing into Havana harbor with its cargo, the *Tecora* remained offshore. Under cover of night, the African captives were loaded into small boats and taken to Cuba. Then they marched inland where they remained in barracoons before going to the auction block.

All this secrecy was necessary because Spain and England had agreed to work together to outlaw the slave trade. Bringing slaves into the Spanish colony of Cuba was, therefore, illegal. The slave traders could lose their heads if they were caught. However, there was no law preventing Africans who were already slaves on the island of Cuba from being sold by one owner to another at auction. Thus, Cinqué and the other captives were smuggled onto the island, kept in confinement, then sold in Havana's slave mart as if they had always been slaves.

Barracoons were huts that were used to temporarily hold slaves until the next leg of their journey. Joseph Cinqué was placed in a slave barracoon like this one.

A Ship Called *Amistad*

In June 1839, Cinqué was purchased in Havana by José Ruiz, who also bought forty-eight other slaves at a price of $450 each. His associate Pedro Montes purchased four children—three girls and a boy—from the same ship. By bribing government officials in Havana, Montes and Ruiz received passports verifying that all fifty-three slaves had been Spanish residents of Cuba and could be moved to another part of the island.[5]

Ruiz and Montes then transported the slaves to the ship *Amistad*, which was under the command of Ramón Ferrer. With a crew of two sailors, a cook named Celistino, and a cabin boy named Antonio, the ship set sail for Puerto

Dangers of the Slave Trade

By 1839, when Cinqué was taken from Africa, the slave trade had become illegal. The governments of Britain, Spain and the United States—major slave trading countries in the past—were trying to stamp out whatever trade still existed. British patrol ships cruised along the coast of West Africa looking for slave trading ships. But there were not many of these patrol boats and the slave trade continued. US slave ships operating out of New Orleans, for example, brought slaves to South America and the Caribbean islands. But in 1839, the same year as the *Amistad* incident, the British patrol ship *Buzzard* captured two American slavers, or ships used to transport slaves. The two vessels were escorted to New York, where slavery was illegal and slave captains were tried in court.

Príncipe on another part of the island. There, the Africans would go to work on a Cuban plantation, growing and harvesting sugarcane.

Although the Africans were not chained during the day, they received little food or water during the hot, three-hundred-mile trip along the Cuban coast. When one of them, Burnah, tried to get something more to drink, he was flogged. Cinqué began to worry that there would not be enough food for the captives to survive the trip. He tried to communicate with the cook through sign language, since Cinqué could not speak Spanish and Celistino could not understand any African dialect. The Spanish cook simply smiled and indicated that some of the captives would be killed and fed to the others. It was a cruel joke, but Cinqué did not realize that the cook was joking.

Cinqué was horrified. He decided that the time had come to take action. On June 30, as the *Amistad* made its way along the Cuban coast, he stole a nail from the ship's stores. That night, as the slaves lay in chains, Cinqué used the nail to unlock his manacles (shackles for the hands). Then he released the other captives. Together with another African named Grabeau, Cinqué led the men to the place where the ship's weapons were stored. They helped themselves to knives and hatchets, then stormed the main deck where the captain was sleeping. Before Ferrer had time to defend himself, he had been overpowered and killed. The former slaves also turned on Celistino and butchered him with their hatchets. Although the rest of the crew escaped, Ruiz and Montes were captured. They decided to surrender. The *Amistad* now belonged to the Africans.

Joseph Cinqué led an attack on the crew members of the *Amistad* because he believed the lives of the Africans were in imminent danger.

Primary Source—A Newspaper Account of the *Amistad* Revolt

On coming along side [the **Amistad*****] a number of negroes were discovered on her deck, and twenty or thirty more were on the beach—two white men came forward and claimed the protection of the officer. The schooner proved to be the "Amistad" . . . with 54 blacks and two passengers on board; the former, four nights after they were out, rose and murdered the captain and three of the crew; they then took possession of the vessel with the intention of returning to the coast of Africa . . . [T]he vessel was steered by Pedro Montes for New Providence, the negroes being under the impression that she was steering for the coast of Africa . . . The situation of the two whites was all this time truly deplorable, being treated with the greatest severity . . . The negroes were found in communication with shore, where they laid in a fresh supply of water, and were on the point of sailing again for the coast of Africa. They had a good supply of money with them, some of which it is likely was taken by the people on the beach.—After they were disarmed, and sent on board from the beach, the ringleader jumped overboard with three hundred doubloons about him, the property of the captain, all of which he succeeded in loosing from his person and then permitted himself to be captured.***[6]

—*From the* New London Gazette, *published on August 26, 1839.*

The Africans Head Northward

The Africans wanted to return home to Mende country. Cinqué reasoned that the best way to get home was to sail toward the rising sun—that is, to the east. Because neither he nor any of the other Africans knew how to sail the ship, Cinqué forced Montes to chart a course to Sierra Leone in Africa.

Montes, however, had other plans. While heading east during part of the day, Montes steered the ship northward toward the North American coast at night. He hoped that it would be spotted by English or American sailing vessels and rescued. Meanwhile, the *Amistad* was running desperately short of food and water. Some of the Africans became so thirsty that they began drinking medicines that were stored on board and died. The Africans on board the *Amistad* tried to hail passing ships. But the other ships' captains were usually scared off when they drew close and saw black men armed with knives and hatchets.

Gradually, the *Amistad* sailed northward on a zigzag course that roughly paralleled the North American coast. Word of this strange ship with its African crew began to reach harbors along the continent. In August 1839, the *Amistad* finally anchored off the coast of Long Island, New York. Cinqué did not know where he had stopped. But the men needed food desperately, so he and some of the others went ashore to find food and water. Although they frightened most of the residents who saw them, Cinqué and the others were able to buy some supplies with money they had found aboard the *Amistad*.

But the activities of Cinqué and his men had not gone unobserved. They encountered a small party led by Captain

An engraving depicting the *Amistad* revolt. The slaves on board killed the captain and the cook of the Spanish schooner.

Henry Green, who had heard about the ship and hoped to capture it. Cinqué wanted them to take the *Amistad* back to Africa. Meanwhile, out at sea, an American patrol boat, the USS *Washington*, under the command of Lieutenant Thomas R. Gedney, had spotted the *Amistad*. The men of the *Washington* had seen the Africans onshore, where they appeared to be engaged in smuggling. Gedney sent a few armed sailors, led by D.D. Porter and Richard W. Meade, in a small boat to board the *Amistad*.

Reaching the ship, they encountered some of the Africans who had not gone onshore. They were quickly disarmed. Then Meade and his men found Ruiz and Montes below decks. In broken English, Ruiz explained what had happened—or at least, his side of the story. He claimed that the Africans were slaves being legally transported in Cuba, when they had revolted and killed the captain of the ship. According to Ruiz, what they had done was nothing less than mutiny and murder.

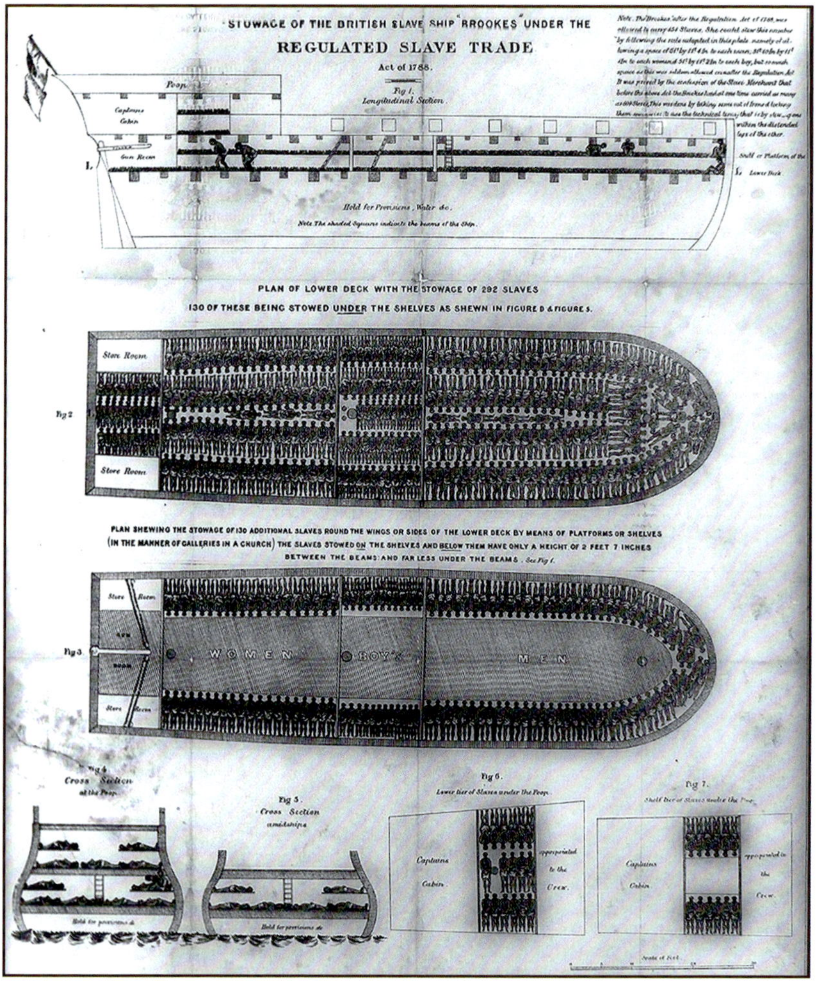

Slaves being brought across the Atlantic were packed together as tightly as possible. Disease quickly spread throughout the close quarters and many died along the journey.

While the Africans were being held on board the *Amistad*, some of the American sailors went to shore. There, they captured Cinqué and the rest of his men. When he was brought on board the ship, Cinqué broke free and jumped over the side of the boat. He was finally captured and imprisoned aboard the *Amistad*. As the leader of the other Africans, he tried to spark a revolt so they could return home. But Lieutenant Gedney quickly removed him to the *Washington*.

Gedney then had to decide what to do with the *Amistad* and the people on board. If the Africans were slaves, as Ruiz claimed, they would be worth some money. Gedney might be able to claim a substantial reward from the government for capturing them and the ship. In New York, however, slavery was illegal, so his claim might not be allowed. In nearby Connecticut, on the other hand, slavery was still legal. Perhaps this is what persuaded Gedney to bring the ship to New London, Connecticut, on August 27, 1839.

The *Amistad* Ignites a Conflict

The capture of the *Amistad* may have seemed like a routine action by an American naval vessel. But it would rapidly become much more. The cause of Cinqué and the other Africans would quickly be taken up by the abolitionists, who wanted to bring an end to slavery throughout the United States. A series of celebrated court cases would result, ending in a landmark judgment by the United States Supreme Court. The *Amistad* case would help polarize feelings between Northern free states and slaveholding Southern states. The incident would not bring any resolution to the issue of slavery or the slave trade. Instead, it would serve as an important link in the chain of events that would eventually lead to the American Civil War.

CHAPTER 2

The Voyage Across the Atlantic

Slave trading is probably almost as old as human history. In the ancient world, many of those citizens who were conquered in warfare were often sold into slavery. The Egyptians practiced slavery, placing the Jews in bondage until they were led to freedom by Moses. Later the Romans enslaved conquered Germans and Gauls whom they had defeated in battle. Some of the captives became household slaves, cleaning the homes and cooking the meals for well-to-do Romans. Others became field hands, laboring for hours under the hot Italian sun in large wheat fields. They sowed the crops, harvested them, and then ground wheat into flour to make bread for the Romans. The Greek philosopher Aristotle explained, "A slave is a living possession."[1] Indeed, without these slaves, the Greek or the Roman economy could not have functioned.

After the fall of Rome in the fifth century, slavery continued. In wars between tribes, there were winners and losers, conquerors and slaves. These slaves were sold at giant markets in European cities such as Verdun, Arles, and Lyons. Meanwhile, in North Africa, Muslim armies began to sweep across the continent. Although the Koran, or Muslim holy book, expressly forbade enslaving fellow Muslims, it did not prevent making slaves of infidels, or non-Muslims. In the eighth century, Arab soldiers crossed the Mediterranean Sea into Spain. They defeated the Visigoths who lived there, and these people became slaves of the Muslims.

The Arabs also extended their power southward from the Sahara Desert into central Africa. They came into contact with black African tribes, whose culture they regarded as inferior to their own. The Muslims made slaves of some of these people. Then they brought them to North Africa to dig in copper mines or to work sugarcane plantations.

During the thirteenth century, explained historian Hugh Thomas, "Moorish traders were to be found offering black slaves from Guinea [in Africa] at fairs . . . in northern Portugal; and blacks bought in North Africa were being sold in Cadiz [Spain] at the end of that century."[2] Thus, the Muslims extended black slavery to Spain and Portugal.

Portugal Controls the Slave Trade

By this period, however, Arab influence on the Spanish peninsula was in decline. Throughout the Middle Ages, Christian kings had gradually driven back the Moorish (Arab) invaders. By the fifteenth century, Arabs occupied only a small area in the southern part of Spain. Meanwhile, the power of the Portuguese and Spanish rulers had increased.

Portuguese explorers, under the direction of Prince Henry the Navigator, sailed southward along the African coast. They hoped to discover new sources of gold rumored to lie somewhere in the interior. The Portuguese landed at the mouth of the Senegal River, established settlements in the area that became known as Sierra Leone, and eventually

Slavery had been a practice for thousands of years. Here, a woman is being sold as a slave to the Romans.

reached the Benin and Congo rivers. However, they encountered powerful African empires that prevented them from penetrating very far inland. Disease and fear of the unknown also kept the Portuguese along the coast. There, they traded with the African empires for ivory, pepper, and gold. Beginning in the mid-fifteenth century, the Portuguese also began trading in something else, which they considered just as valuable as gold itself—black gold, or slaves.

Slavery had existed in Africa long before the arrival of the Portuguese. Prisoners taken in the tribal wars on the continent were often sold as slaves at huge fairs in what is now Senegal and Gambia in West Africa. But slavery at that time did not mean that a person was forced into a harsh, brutalized existence. "With us," wrote Olaudah Equiano, "they do no more work than other members of the community, even their masters; their food, clothing and lodging were nearly the same as theirs. . . Some of these slaves have even slaves under them as their own property, and for their own use."[3]

As Portuguese traders arrived on the scene, the nature of slavery gradually changed. The Portuguese had already enslaved Moorish soldiers as they had been driven off the Spanish peninsula. Now they acquired African slaves—first by the hundreds, then by the thousands, and finally, by the tens of thousands. Some of these African slaves went to work in the households of wealthy families in Portugal. There, owning a slave came to be considered a symbol of wealth. But many other slaves were taken to the sugar plantations in southern Portugal, on the island of Madeira in the Atlantic Ocean, and at São Tomé in the Gulf of Guinea. Here, they were forced to do backbreaking labor, often for long hours each day. Slaves were no longer treated in the

Slaves had long been a part of African society by the time European slave traders arrived, but the Europeans treated slaves with much more brutality.

way that Olaudah Equiano described. Instead, they became property to be used in any way their masters wished.

To acquire these slaves, the Portuguese ships brought with them trade goods from Europe. These found a ready market among the African tribes. Trade goods included fine cloth from the Netherlands, brass bracelets from Germany, glass beads from Italy, knives and swords from Spain, and wine from the Canary Islands.[4] A lucrative trade developed, enriching merchants in many parts of Europe.

Slavery in the New World

While the Portuguese developed their trade empire along the African coast, Spain was establishing its own empire in the Americas. Christopher Columbus planted the Spanish flag in the Caribbean Sea on islands that included Hispaniola and Cuba. A few years later, conquistadors such as Hernán Cortés and Francisco Pizarro added vast regions to the territory claimed by the Spanish Crown in Mexico and Peru. As Spanish settlers went to live in the New World, they tried to force the native American Indian populations into service on their plantations and *haciendas*, or large estates. But the Indians were indifferent workers. They were also exposed to fatal diseases, such as smallpox, which the Spanish brought with them. The Indians had no immunity to these diseases, and they died by the thousands.

Therefore, Spain still needed a large supply of new workers for its American colonies. Laborers were needed not only to plant sugarcane on the large plantations being staked out in South America, but also to dig for gold and silver in mines. In 1510 African slaves began arriving in Spain's American empire. Meanwhile, they were also being transported to the Portuguese colony of Brazil to work the

Slaves process sugarcane on the Spanish island of Hispaniola in the Caribbean Sea.

huge sugar plantations there. During the sixteenth century, the demand for slaves grew until it seemed as if the Spanish and Portuguese colonies could not exist without them.

But no matter how many slaves arrived in the Americas, there never seemed to be enough of them to work the growing number of plantations. As a Spanish official in Lima, Peru, said in 1646: "The shortage of blacks threatens the total ruin of the entire kingdom, for the black slave is the basis of the hacienda and the source of all wealth which this realm produces."[5]

During this same period—from 1625 to 1650—approximately two hundred thousand slaves were imported to the Americas.[6] The life they were forced to lead was extremely harsh. Africans were routinely beaten by overseers and forced to work almost around the clock during the long sugarcane harvests. From the fields, the slaves transported the cane to sugar mills. There, the juice was ground out of the cane, boiled, skimmed, and cooled into rough sugar crystals. In the process, many slaves lost limbs in the machinery of the mill. Slaves were not expected to live long under the brutal conditions of the sugarcane plantations. Therefore, a fresh supply of slaves was constantly needed.

From the Americas, the rough sugar was transported to Europe, where it was refined. As the population of Europe grew, the demand increased for sugar to be used as a sweetener for tea, coffee, and milk, or as an ingredient in chocolate and other candy. Thus, a triangular trade developed. European ships brought trade goods to Africa in return for slaves. Then the slaves were transported to the Americas to work on the sugar plantations. From there, raw sugar was carried back to Europe to be refined and used as a sweetener.

The Lure of Black Gold

Portugal and Spain were not the only countries with colonies in the Americas. Great Britain and France also established empires that demanded slaves. During the seventeenth and eighteenth centuries, British and French merchants supplied these slaves from trading posts in West Africa. These were located along the Ivory Coast, which was a rich source of ivory tusks, and the Gold Coast, an area with large gold deposits. The British referred to this entire area as Guinea. Some of the gold brought back to England was minted into coins, which were known as *guineas*.

But it was black gold—slaves—that made up the largest percentage of cargo brought out of Africa. British ships from Liverpool, Bristol, and London carried more than two hundred thousand slaves to the Americas between 1740 and 1750. Many of them worked the sugar plantations on the Caribbean islands of Jamaica and Barbados. Meanwhile, the Portuguese, Spanish, and French were also bringing slaves to their colonies. By the end of the eighteenth century, the total number of slaves leaving Africa each year had reached eighty thousand.[7]

In return for these slaves, the English and other traders exchanged a vast assortment of goods with African tribal chiefs. In addition to cloth and brass items, the chiefs were now interested in muskets to defend their lands as well as iron bars that could be melted down and shaped into farm tools. But to obtain these things, they had to supply an ever-increasing number of slaves to fill the demands of the European traders.

As the European colonies expanded, the demand for slaves grew. Here, groups of slaves are loaded onto ships bound for the Americas.

The Role of African Slave Traders

Cinqué's long ordeal began when he was kidnapped by African slave traders near his village. Kidnapping was a primary method of supplying the large numbers of slaves requested by European merchants. In some cases, the victim may have owed a debt he could not pay. This may have been the reason Cinqué was taken. Others were enslaved as punishment for a crime, such as adultery, murder, or repeated thefts. Still others sold their children into slavery because they could not afford to feed them. Warfare also

Primary Source—A Young Boy is Kidnapped Into Slavery

I was born in Dukandarra, in Guinea, about the year 1729. . . . A detachment from the enemy came to my father and informed him, that the whole army was encamped not far out of his dominions, and would invade the territory and deprive his people of their liberties and rights, if he did not comply with the following terms. These were to pay them a large sum of money, three hundred fat cattle, and a great number of goats, sheep, asses, etc.

My father told the messenger he would comply rather than that his subjects should be deprived of their rights and privileges . . . We left our dwellings in succession, and my father's company went on first. We directed our course for a large shrub plain, some distance off, where we intended to conceal ourselves from the approaching enemy. . . . [The enemy] then came to us in the reeds, and the very first salute I had from them was a violent blow on the back part of the head with the fore part of a gun, and at the same time a grasp round the neck. I then had a rope put about my neck, as had all the women in the thicket with me, and were immediately led to my father, who was likewise pinioned and haltered for leading . . . On a certain time I and other prisoners were put on board a canoe, under our master, and rowed away to a vessel belonging to Rhode Island, commanded by Captain Collingwood, and the mate Thomas Mumford. While we were going to the vessel, our master told us all to appear to the best possible advantage for sale.[8]

— Venture Smith gave this account of his capture and enslavement at the age of six.

served as an important means of acquiring slaves. Indeed, some tribes may have initiated wars in order to capture their enemies so that they could be sold on the coast to the slave merchants.

Once a man like Cinqué was captured, he might begin a long trek before arriving at one of the European trading posts on the African coast. Cinqué, for example, was sold by his captors to a tribal prince, who then took him to the barracoon of Pedro Blanco. Other Africans reported being exchanged many times before reaching a ship bound for the Americas. Dr. Alexander Falconbridge, who was a surgeon aboard slave ships, reported being told by a black woman:

> As she was on her return home one evening, from some neighbors to whom she had been making a visit by invitation, she was kidnapped and notwithstanding she was big with child, she was sold for a slave. This transaction happened a considerable way up the country and she had passed through the hands of several purchasers before she reached the ship.[9]

Many slaves were sold at trade fairs. Black traders might set off from a European trading post on the coast with as many as twenty or thirty canoes. Each was large enough to carry up to forty slaves. The traders hoped to barter for them, according to Dr. Falconbridge, by putting such goods . . . on board as they expect will be wanted for the purchase of the number of slaves they intend to buy. When their loading is completed they commence their voyage with colors flying and music playing and in about ten or eleven days generally return . . . with full cargoes. As soon as the canoes arrive at

African traders loaded their canoes full of captives and brought them to trade fairs to be sold.

the trader's landing place, the [slaves] are cleaned and oiled with palm oil and on the following day they are exposed for sale to the [ship] captains.[10]

Sometimes no ships were docked in port, and the slaves had to be housed in a barracoon. Cinqué was confined at Pedro Blanco's fort in Lomboko. It was a stout fortress with high towers, small huts for Blanco's men, and a large home for the trader. Cinqué was kept in a wooden building with the other slaves awaiting shipment to America.

Other barracoons were different. At the British fortress of Cabo Corso Castle on the Gold Coast, for example, slaves were kept in stone vaults below the ground. The only air came through an iron grating on the surface. As many as a thousand slaves might be kept below ground, chained together, before being put on board a ship. As they awaited transport, slaves might easily contract a disease and die.

Once the ships arrived, the next stage of the slaves' ordeal began. Before any was purchased, each would be carefully examined by a surgeon, such as Dr. Falconbridge. For this examination, the Africans would be stripped naked. The surgeon would test their limbs, examine their genitals for any disease, look into their eyes, and open their mouths to make sure their teeth were not rotten.

Once the slaves were purchased, another ritual occurred. As one slave captain explained:

> Then we mark'd the slaves we had bought in the breast, or shoulder, with a hot iron, having the letter of the ship's name on it, the place being before anointed with a little palm oil, which caused but little pain, the mark being usually well in four or five days, appearing very plain and white after.[11]

Primary Source— The Slave Trade in Africa

Those sold by the Blacks are for the most part prisoners of war, taken either in fight, or pursuit, or in the incursions they make into their enemies territories; others stolen away by their own countrymen; and some there are, who will sell their own children, kindred, or neighbours . . . The kings are so absolute, that upon any slight pretense of offences committed by their subjects, they order them to be sold for slaves, without regard to rank, or possession . . . Abundance of little Blacks of both sexes are also stolen away by their neighbours, when found abroad on the roads, or in the woods . . . In times of dearth and famine, abundance of those people will sell themselves, for a maintenance, and to prevent starving . . .

Th[e] barbarous usage of those unfortunate wretches, makes it appear, that the fate of such as are bought and transported from the coast to America, or other parts of the world, by Europeans, is less deplorable, than that of those who end their days in their native country; for aboard ships all possible care is taken to preserve and subsist them for the interest of the owners, and when sold in America, the same motive ought to prevail with their masters to use them well, that they may live the longer, and do them more service.[12]

—*John Barbot, who worked for the French Royal African Company, described the African slave trade in 1682.*

The slaves, who had been branded like horses or cattle, were then loaded aboard ship to begin the next leg of their long journey.

A Journey Through the Middle Passage

For Africans like Cinqué, the most difficult part of the journey may have occurred as their ship began to pull away from the African coast. Cinqué realized that he would probably never see his home or his wife and three children again. For some of the captives, this terrible realization was too much to bear. They threw themselves overboard into the harbor, where they were often eaten alive by sharks. Apparently, even a terrible death seemed better than being separated from home and family. Since they had no idea where they were going or what terrible things might happen to them, they committed suicide rather than face the horrors of the unknown.

The rest of the captives, however, began a long voyage to the Americas. The trip to America was called the Middle Passage—the middle part of the triangular trade. In good weather, this trip might last from thirty to fifty days. The voyage was much longer if the ship encountered storms crossing the Atlantic. Because the Africans had never been to sea, they usually became violently seasick. Their misery was made even worse by the terrible conditions in which they were forced to live during the voyage. Cinqué was one of five hundred slaves crammed below decks in the ship *Tecora*. All the men were chained together in a small area where it was impossible for them to stand up. There was very little fresh air, except for the breezes that might come through the portholes. Dr. Falconbridge explained how such conditions often affected the slaves:

Some African captives jumped off the slave ships, preferring to drown or be eaten by sharks rather than be separated from their families.

> During the voyages I made, I was frequently witness to the fatal effects of this exclusion of fresh air . . . Some wet and blowing weather having occasioned the port-holes to be shut and the grating to be covered, fluxes and fevers among the Negroes ensued. While they were in this situation, I frequently went down among them till at length their room became so extremely hot as to be only bearable for a very short time. . . .The deck, that is the floor of their rooms, was so covered with the blood and mucus which had proceeded from them in consequence of . . . [sickness], that it resembled a slaughter-house.[13]

Since the slavers got paid by the head, it was in their best interests to deliver as many people as possible to the Americas. Nevertheless, many Africans died from diseases such as dysentery, smallpox, and dehydration. Not only the captives, but also the crews of the slave ships often complained of too little water. "Much of what there was became foul during the course of the voyage, growing thick with algae," explained historian Madeleine Burnside. "Only recently has dehydration been understood as the underlying medical cause of the depression so often noted in the African captives."[14]

The captives were not kept below deck all the time. The men were brought on the top deck two or three times a day to be fed. However, they were securely chained together to prevent mutinies. Women and children were kept separate from the men. Unlike the male slaves, they were not chained because they posed less of a threat to the crew of the slave ship.

Even with these precautions, rebellions did occur. But they were usually put down by the heavily armed crew. Sometimes the leaders of the rebellion would jump overboard and face drowning rather than the punishment that awaited them. Frequently, Burnside wrote, "The participating slaves were flogged and their leaders killed. Many slave ship captains also believed it prudent to dismember publicly the leaders of a revolt, letting their fate serve as a warning to the others."[15] In one case, the leader of a revolt had his right hand cut off, then his left, and finally, he was beheaded.

Slave ships headed for the Americas might put in at one of the ports where large slave auctions were held. These included Rio de Janeiro, Brazil; Cartagena, on the northern coast of South America; or Havana, Cuba. From these slave marts the slaves were transported to plantations to spend the rest of their lives under the whip of a harsh overseer.

The Harsh Plantation Life

Cuba was a lush, tropical island crisscrossed with huge sugar and coffee plantations. No other island in the Caribbean grew as many tons of sugar each year as this small Spanish colony. What made the enormous sugarcane crop possible, however, were thousands and thousands of slaves. As one Spanish governor-general on the island put it, "If there is no slave labor, the island's wealth will disappear within a few years. . . ."[16]

As a slave on a Cuban plantation, Cinqué's life would no longer be his own. He would become a piece of property that could be ordered to do anything by his master, sold whenever his master wanted, and severely punished if he should ever disobey. James Thompson was owned by several masters before becoming a field worker and a house servant

Slave mutinies like the one depicted here occurred occasionally but were rarely successful. The slaves were usually overpowered by the crew and severely punished.

Primary Source: A Slave Being Sold at Market

Many merchants and planters now come on board . . . examined us attentively made us jump, and pointed to the land signifying we were to go there. We thought by this we should be eaten by these ugly men . . . there was much dread and trembling among us, and nothing but bitter cries to be heard all the night . . . at last the white people got some old slaves from the land to pacify us. They told us we were not to be eaten, but to work and were soon to go on land where we should see many of our country people. This report eased us much; and sure enough, soon after we landed, there came to us Africans of all languages. We were conducted immediately to the merchant's yard, where we were all pent up together like so many sheep . . . we were sold after their usual manner, which is this: On a given signal (as the beat of a drum), the buyers rush at once into the yard where the slaves are confined, and make choice of that parcel they like best. The noise and clamor with which this is attended, and the eagerness visible In the countenances of the buyers, serve to increase the apprehension of the terrified Africans.[17]

—Olaudah Equiano recounted his experience as a slave arriving in Barbados.

on a coffee plantation. He recalled that, each day, the old mistress of the plantation would come into the kitchen and "strike me with a stick for some real or imaginary fault . . ." She was never satisfied with him, although he not only cooked for the family, but after his household duties were done, he also picked coffee in the fields. After she died, his situation grew even worse:

> Her son and daughter continually ill-used me; the latter would frequently take a stick out of the fire, and break it over my head; and the former one day gave me such a severe beating with his *manati* (a whip made of the skin of the sea-cow) that I was three days in the hospital.

While he worked on the plantation, Thompson fell in love with a woman and asked for permission to marry her. Slaves were not allowed to marry without the consent of their masters. But permission was refused. Instead, Thompson and his girlfriend were placed side by side on the ground and each given two hundred fifty lashes:

> After this, we had irons placed on our feet, with a chain connecting them suspended from the waist. A collar with three hooks was placed round our necks and a coupling chain secured to each collar. Thus linked together, we worked in the field for two years and a half, being every night and during the hours of rest on the Sundays and festivals, confined in the stocks.[18]

A similar fate most likely awaited Cinqué, unless he could escape.

The American Slave Trade

Slavery had been legal for thousands of years. But during the eighteenth century attitudes toward the slave trade began to change. In England, a group of determined reformers decided that the terrible practice must come to an end. For decades, they worked to achieve this goal. At first, they met with little success, but eventually they rallied the majority of England behind them. By 1839, when Cinqué was captured, the slave trade had been outlawed.

Great Britain Tries to End the Slave Trade

The reform movement was led by Thomas Clarkson, a founder of the Society for the Abolition of the Slave Trade. He published pamphlets based on the information he gathered from talking to seamen who were involved in the slave trade.

Another leader of the reform movement was the brilliant politician William Wilberforce, whose stirring speeches in Parliament (the British legislature) condemned the work of the English merchants who had sold so many Africans

William Wilberforce was an English politician who played a major role in abolishing the slave trade in the British Empire.

into slavery. "Africa, Africa," Wilberforce said in one of his speeches, "your sufferings have been the theme that has arrested and engages my heart. Your sufferings no tongue can express, no language impart."[1]

At first, there was enormous opposition to ending the slave trade because so many merchants were growing rich from it. Still, the reformers persisted. Gradually, they won over public opinion by exposing the cruelties of slavery. In 1807 Parliament passed a law that outlawed the slave trade in the British colonies.

After passage of the law, English slave stations in Africa were abandoned, and the navy began to patrol the African coast to stop the flow of slaves to the Americas. The British realized, however, that it was not enough simply to eliminate the slave trade in their own empire; other nations had to do the same thing. Under pressure from England, whose powerful navy controlled the sea, Spain and Portugal decided to eliminate the slave trade, too. They also gave British ships the right to stop any Portuguese or Spanish vessels suspected of carrying slaves. Thus, the Portuguese ship *Tecora* was violating the law by bringing Cinqué and the other Africans to Cuba. The ship could have been stopped, its cargo confiscated, and its captain hauled into court in Cuba to stand trial for engaging in the slave trade.

Slave trading had become a risky business. But the British and their allies had so few ships to patrol the waters that many slavers made it to Cuba without being caught. In 1836, just three years before Cinqué's arrival, sixty thousand slaves had been brought there.[2] Why did so many slave ships get through? As historian Warren Howard put it: "The fundamental answer is that none of the nations trying to suppress the trade was serious enough to employ adequate naval patrols . . . [T]he much-publicized British African squadron never had half as many cruisers as it needed. . . ."[3] And in the Caribbean, Spain and Great Britain employed very few ships to stop the slavers.

Nevertheless, slave merchants did not flout the law too openly. Once they arrived off the island of Cuba, the slaves were taken on shore under cover of night. Then they were hidden in confinement areas for short periods before being taken to the Havana slave auctions. All this deception was to make it look as if the slaves were already employed at a coffee or sugar plantation and were simply being sold to another plantation owner. Although the international slave trade was illegal, slavery on the island of Cuba was perfectly legal, and slave trade on the island itself was protected by law.

Of course, the Spanish authorities were not really fooled. But they received large bribes to look the other way. Indeed, one governor-general was rumored to have put a half ounce of gold in his pocket every time a slave reached Cuba safely. As Nicholas Trist, the United States consul in Havana, explained in 1839,

> The truth of the existing state of things here, in relation to the slave-trade, can be condensed into one sentence. It is a pursuit denounced in every possible way by the LAW—by law FOREIGN made and FOREIGN imposed—and supported by an overwhelming PUBLIC OPINION. . . .[4]

Trist might have added that American merchants were also participating in the slave trade. The United States, unlike Spain and Portugal, had never given the British

Cuban farmers began planting tobacco in the eighteenth century. Plantations like the one shown here used slave labor to grow and harvest the crop.

permission to stop and search its ships. Sleek merchant vessels, manufactured in American ports such as Baltimore, Maryland, were sent south to Havana. From there, they were used by Spanish and Portuguese slavers on their trips to Africa, often sailing with an American captain and under an American flag to elude the British patrols. Thus American businessmen, as well as their counterparts in Cuba, made huge profits from the slave trade. Some of these slaves were also being transported from Havana to the United States to work on the huge cotton plantations in the South.

Slavery and the Economy of the South

The schooner *Amistad* that brought Cinqué and his companions to North America had originally been built in the Baltimore shipyards. But the ship was hardly being used for the purposes its builders had intended. As the *Amistad* zigzagged northward, reports of this strange ship reached the mainland, causing fear among Southerners who heard that blacks were in control of the ship. If this were true, it posed a threat to a Southern society that was based on the institution of black slavery.

African slavery had been introduced to the American colonies in 1619 when a Dutch ship arrived in Jamestown, Virginia, with twenty Africans to be sold as slaves. However, slavery grew slowly because Southern farm owners relied on indentured servants to help them work their land. These impoverished people, mainly Europeans, sold their services for a fixed period of time, in return for passage to America and a place to live. As tobacco plantations developed in Virginia, Maryland, and North Carolina, indentured servants remained the primary labor force working the fields.

The first ship carrying twenty African slaves arrived in Jamestown in 1619.

During the latter part of the seventeenth century, however, fewer of England's poor came to North America. Jobs were more plentiful at home. Gradually, Southern planters began to rely more heavily on black slaves to work the tobacco fields as well as the huge rice plantations that developed in North and South Carolina. At first, white and black field hands worked side by side. Many blacks were freed after a specific period of time, just like indentured servants. They then bought their own land, and generally enjoyed many of the same rights as white plantation owners.

The Power of the Plantation Owners

Over the next century, the demand for slaves on Southern plantations continued to grow. Many of these slaves were supplied by the Royal African Company, whose sailing ships transported them from Africa. American merchants also participated in the slave trade. Biographer Edward Ball described the activities of one of his ancestors, Henry Laurens—a co-owner of the Charleston, South Carolina, merchant firm of Austin and Laurens: "In the ten years between 1751 and 1761," Ball wrote, "George Austin and Henry Laurens brought sixty-one slave galleys to the Charleston wharfs—the largest number of any slave importer in the city. . . ."[5] Indeed, from the beginning of the eighteenth century, more than 40 percent of all the slaves arriving in North America came through Charleston.[6]

In the Southern states, the proportion of blacks in the population increased dramatically. Between 1680 and 1750, the number grew from 7 percent to 44 percent in Virginia, for example, and from 17 percent to 61 percent in South Carolina.[7] In the North, by contrast, there were never many slaves. Most Northerners owned small farms and grew only

Slave Trade in the Eighteenth Century

During the eighteenth century, the slave traders brought an increasing number of slaves to North America. From ten thousand slaves in the decade of the 1720s, the number rose to forty thousand in the 1740s and seventy thousand in the 1760s.[8] The slaves worked on rice and indigo plantations in South Carolina and Georgia. They also planted and harvested tobacco in Virginia, Maryland, and Florida.

enough food to feed themselves. The Northern colonies did not develop huge tobacco and rice plantations, which needed large numbers of laborers. However, merchants in the North did not hesitate to participate in the slave trade, which offered huge profits for anyone willing to sail the Atlantic. Ship captains from ports such as Boston, Massachusetts; New London, Connecticut; and Newport, Rhode Island; regularly sailed to Africa with casks of rum manufactured in New England. They would trade this rum with African chiefs for slaves—two hundred gallons per slave in the middle of the eighteenth century.[9] Then they would take the slaves to the Caribbean islands, where they would be sold. Part of the profit would be invested in molasses, which would be taken back to New England and used to make rum. In addition to this triangular trade, New England merchants also took lumber and fish to the West Indies, where they were sold for slaves who were then transported to the Southern colonies.

As the number of slaves in the South increased, the laws that governed them gradually became much harsher. Perhaps white Southerners grew worried about having such a large slave population in their midst—a population that looked different and had different customs. Slaves might revolt against their masters. A series of laws was enacted in the Southern states that institutionalized slavery and ensured that black slaves would remain in a subordinate position. Slaves were expected to remain in slavery for life and plantation owners were encouraged not to free them. In addition, slaves were not allowed to carry weapons or to leave the plantation without written permission. Any slaves who did not obey their masters could expect severe punishment. Historian Peter Kolchin explained:

Many slaves on plantations were regularly whipped and beaten by their masters or overseers.

Primary Source—Slave Punishment

I will relate . . . what I heard Mr. George Lee's overseer Morgan say the other day that he had often done to Negroes himself and had found useful. He said that whipping of any kind does them no good, for they will laugh at your greatest severity. But he told us he had invented [something] and proved [its] effectiveness by trying [it] several times. For sullenness, obstinacy, or laziness, he says, take a Negro, strip him, and tie him fast to a post. Then take a sharp curry comb and curry him severely until he is well scraped; then call a boy with some dry hay and make the boy rub him down for several minutes; and then salt him and release him. He will . . . attend to his business afterwards![10]

—A tutor from the North, teaching on a Southern plantation, described the treatment of slaves.

> Born in violence, slavery survived by the lash. Beginning with the initial slave trade that tore Africans away from everything they knew and sent them in chains to a distant land to toil for strangers, every stage of master-slave relations depended either directly or indirectly on physical coercion. The routine functioning of Southern farms and plantations rested on the authority of the owners . . . supported by the state, to inflict pain on their human property. Plenty of pain was inflicted.[11]

One slave named Madison Jefferson repeatedly tried to escape from the plantation where he worked. Once, when he was recaptured, his master told him that he would be brutally beaten. Jefferson received fifty lashes and was chained at night but was released to work in the fields during the day. Plantation workers on the large plantations were supervised by black slave drivers who operated under the direction of a white overseer, or the master himself on smaller plantations. Men and women who could not do their work were given twenty-five to thirty lashes over their clothes. If this did not convince them to work harder, the overseer would inflict another flogging of sixty to one hundred lashes. Even pregnant women were lashed, Jefferson recalled.[12]

The Growth of Slavery in the South

In 1776 the American colonies declared their independence from Great Britain. Over the next few years, they fought a war to ensure their freedom. For many of the patriots, the notion of individual liberty seemed inconsistent with the practice of slavery. Following the American victory in the Revolutionary War, the Northern states gradually abolished slavery. In the South, however, slavery remained. It formed the bedrock of the plantation system.

At the Constitutional Convention of 1787, several Southern delegates threatened that their states would not join any new federal union if the slave trade were not protected. The Constitution does not mention slavery by name, but it does contain a compromise worked out by the Founding Fathers at the Constitutional Convention. It states that "the Migration or Importation of such Persons as any of the States now existing shall think proper to admit, shall not be prohibited by the Congress prior to the Year one thousand eight hundred and eight. . ." This clause refers to the slave trade—that is, bringing slaves into the United States, which was not to be ended until 1808. The Constitution also protected slave owners whose slaves ran away. It stated that they will "be delivered up on Claim of the Party to whom such Service or Labour may be due."

Although Southern delegates made every effort to protect the institution of slavery, it was actually beginning to decline among the Southern states along the East Coast. Tobacco growing had gradually exhausted the soil of the plantations. It was no longer as valuable a cash crop.

Then, in 1793, a young tutor named Eli Whitney invented a device that would enable slaves to separate more rapidly the fiber from the seed of short staple cotton. This was the only type of cotton that could flourish on plantations that were not located along the coast. The cotton gin, as the device was called, led directly to the development of cotton plantations in states such as Arkansas, Alabama, Mississippi, and Louisiana. In the past, it had taken a slave

With the invention of the cotton gin, the production of cotton surged and the need for slaves skyrocketed.

an entire day to clean a pound of cotton. With a hand cotton gin, a slave could clean fifty pounds of cotton a day; larger power-driven gins could clean a thousand pounds of cotton daily. From 138,000 pounds of cotton produced in the South in 1792, production rose to over 17 million pounds by 1800.[13] Eventually, cotton would become America's biggest export. The demand was greatest in England, where mills turned cotton into cloth. But New England mill owners also depended on Southern-grown cotton for the domestic cloth industry.

As cotton growing expanded, the demand for slaves began to grow again. In the three years before the abolition of the international slave trade in 1808, 202 vessels came into Charleston Harbor carrying slaves. After 1808, when the external slave trade was formally abolished in the United States, an illegal trade in slaves continued. Slaves were brought into the United States from Galveston Island in Texas, which was still part of Spanish Mexico. Another trading center was Amelia Island, off northern Florida. The pirates Jean and Pierre Lafitte sent their ships into the Caribbean from Barataria Bay, south of New Orleans, to hijack slave ships and bring their cargoes illegally into the United States. In 1820 the United States government strengthened the laws against the slave trade, making any violation punishable by death. As a result, the slave trade declined for a time, but increased again a decade later.

By far the largest slave trade took place within the South itself, where it was perfectly legal to buy and sell slaves. Plantation owners in the east no longer needed as many slaves because their soil was exhausted from growing tobacco. They found it very profitable to sell their slaves to planters farther west. As Edward Ball explained, his ancestors were no different. They found selling slaves at auction a profitable business: "It was not unusual in this period to see long columns of black people tramping in chains through the wilderness, on a forced march from South Carolina to the new cotton plantations. The Ball auction was nicely timed to meet the demand."[14]

Meanwhile, the population of Southern slaves was increasing due to the high birthrates among black women and a lower death rate. Slaves were probably treated somewhat better in the South than in the Caribbean or South America, and there were fewer diseases. In 1810, just after the end of the legal slave trade, the slave population stood at just over one million. By 1860, there were almost 4 million slaves in the United States.[15]

Along with Cuba and Brazil, the Southern states were virtually the only areas in the Western Hemisphere where slavery was still legal. Indeed, slavery was so much a part of the Southern economy and society that Southerners felt it was their duty to defend it against any and all threats.

The *Amistad* case posed such a threat. It would ignite a firestorm in the South.

CHAPTER 4

America and the *Amistad*

Although the vast majority of slaves lived in the South, slavery was not only a southern institution. For over a century, New London, Connecticut, had been a center of the triangular trade, bringing thousands of slaves into the United States. In the process, New London merchants grew rich from slavery. Indeed, in August 1839, when the USS *Washington* accompanied the *Amistad* into New London harbor, Connecticut still permitted slavery within its borders.

Shortly after the *Amistad* docked in New London, federal district Judge Andrew T. Judson was notified of the situation. On August 27, he held an inquiry aboard the *Washington* into the facts surrounding the mutiny on the *Amistad* that had led to the death of the captain and the cook. Judge Judson verified from the ship's papers that the *Amistad* had been involved in transporting slaves along the coast of Cuba. He also talked to José Ruiz and Pedro Montes, who claimed to own the slaves. And he interviewed Antonio—a black slave who had belonged to the ship's captain. All of them said that Cinqué had led an illegal mutiny. It appeared that the Africans were guilty of piracy and murder.

After the *Amistad* was captured by Americans, it was brought into the port of New London, Connecticut, where slavery was still legal.

Ruiz and Montes asked that the *Amistad* be handed over to the Spanish authorities. But Judson did not want to make any decision too hastily. He ordered the Africans, thirty-nine adults and four children, to be held for a few weeks in a New Haven, Connecticut, jail. Then they would be taken before the grand jury of the United States circuit court, which was due to meet in Hartford, Connecticut. The grand jury would decide what should happen to them.

The *Amistad* case might have been quietly and quickly handled by the Hartford grand jury, without most people ever hearing about it—except for the presence of one man who had been aboard the *Washington*. His name was Dwight P. Janes, an abolitionist who lived in New London. In an off-the-record conversation with Ruiz, Janes had learned that none of the Africans was really a Cuban slave. They had been brought to the island illegally. This meant that they were free. Janes decided that he must do everything possible to help them regain their freedom. As a strong believer in abolition, he also hoped to turn the *Amistad* incident into a highly publicized event that might help abolish slavery.

Growth of the Abolition Movement

The abolition movement had existed since the eighteenth century, especially among the Quakers of Pennsylvania. Abolitionists strongly believed that slavery and the slave trade were morally wrong and should be stopped immediately. Following the American Revolution, most Northern states gradually abolished slavery, but the institution continued in the South. However, most Northerners felt that slavery should be left alone, not abolished by force. They expected that it would eventually die out as it was doing in the North.

Having little national support for abolition, antislavery advocates began to focus their attention on an alternative. They encouraged Southern planters to free their slaves one by one so the slaves could be resettled in Africa. In 1821 the American Colonization Society founded the territory of Liberia in West Africa. The colony began receiving black settlers a year later. Among the society's early supporters were a young journalist named William Lloyd Garrison and wealthy New York merchants Lewis and Arthur Tappan.

While Liberia was being established, a religious revival movement began to sweep through many parts of America. Religious leaders called on their followers to rededicate themselves to creating a society that would be free from sin and run according to high moral principles. They envisioned a nation that would eliminate the vices of gambling, drinking, adultery, and slavery—for slavery seemed completely opposed to all religious teachings. Men such as Garrison and the Tappan brothers began to realize that colonization would never free the slaves. Only abolition could be successful. In 1831 Garrison began publishing *The Liberator*, which became one of the most powerful abolitionist journals in the country. Although its circulation was always small, its inflammatory language condemning slavery and the plantation system incensed Southerners.

In 1833 Great Britain abolished slavery throughout its colonies in the West Indies. That same year, Garrison, the Tappans, and almost sixty other abolitionists founded the American Anti-Slavery Society. Over the next few years, the society submitted petitions to Congress calling for the abolition of slavery. The society also began a direct mail campaign, sending literature to politicians, ministers, and

William Lloyd Garrison became an outspoken abolitionist who started an antislavery newspaper called *The Liberator*. He and his fellow abolitionists supported the cause of Cinqué and the rest of the captive Africans.

Primary Source—Declaration of Sentiments of the Anti-Slavery Society

We believe and affirm . . . that the slaves ought instantly to be set free and brought under the protection of law. . . .

We further believe and affirm—that all persons of color, who possess the qualifications which are demanded of others, ought to be [allowed] . . . the same privileges . . . as others; and that the paths of preferment of wealth, and of intelligence, should be opened as widely to them as to persons of a white complexion. . . .

We maintain that Congress has a right, and is solemnly bound, to suppress the domestic slave trade between the several States, and to abolish slavery in those portions of our territory which the Constitution has placed under its exclusive jurisdiction [territories, not yet states.][1]

—William Lloyd Garrison wrote this manifesto for the Anti-Slavery Society in 1833.

editors in the North and South, calling for the slaves to be freed.

Southerners vs. Abolitionists

The South reacted furiously to efforts by the Anti-Slavery Society to promote abolition. On July 29, 1835, the people of Charleston, South Carolina, stormed the post office and removed the mail so no abolitionist literature could be distributed. They also burned effigies, or images, of William Lloyd Garrison and Arthur Tappan. Southerners believed that the abolitionists were interfering with something that was none of their business, undermining the foundations of the South's economy.

Plantation owners were already nervous about keeping their slaves under control. Escape attempts were frequent. Historians have estimated that fifty thousand slaves tried to get away each year.[2] Armed patrols regularly roamed the roads, looking for escaped slaves. Slave revolts posed a constant threat to Southerners. They feared that, at any moment, an army of slaves might march down the road to attack their homes—burning, looting, and pillaging.

Rebellions had already occurred a number of times in the past. Along the Stono River near Charleston, a slave named Cato led a small revolt in 1739 that became known as the Stono Rebellion. The slaves attacked a storehouse containing arms and ammunition, then headed south toward Florida, gathering followers as they marched. Once the white militia turned out, however, Cato and his group were cornered. After a bloody battle, most of the slaves were captured and executed.

In 1791 Southern planters reacted with horror to a massive slave uprising in the French colony of Saint-

In the 1830s tensions between the two sides of the slavery argument grew. This illustration depicts a proslavery mob burning down the house of an abolitionist in 1837.

Domingue (Haiti) on the island of Hispaniola in the Caribbean Sea. The hero of that revolution was a free black man named Toussaint L'Ouverture, who conquered the rest of Hispaniola, freed the slaves there, and established an independent government.

A History of Slave Rebellions in the United States

Southerners feared the same thing might happen to them. Although they tried to keep their slaves illiterate, some slaves read about L'Ouverture's exploits. One of them was Gabriel Prosser, a slave in Virginia. In 1800, Prosser, along with his brothers Martin and Solomon, made plans to attack Richmond, the capital of Virginia. They intended to capture a large supply of weapons and take the governor, James Monroe, hostage. However, Prosser's plans were betrayed by two slaves, and he was captured and hanged.

Although the South dealt harshly with slaves who led revolts, this did not stop others from planning to do the same thing. Denmark Vesey had been owned by a slave trader who took him to Haiti, where he learned about L'Ouverture's slave uprising. In 1800 Vesey bought his freedom and set up a carpentry shop in Charleston. Later, he became a member of the African Methodist Episcopal Church, which attracted many black members. This worried white planters, who feared that the church could eventually spark a revolution. In 1821 the authorities closed the church Vesey attended. Although he was a free man with a successful business, Vesey realized that the rights of every black person were in jeopardy as long as white planters controlled the government. He began planning a slave rebellion. Vesey was careful not to reveal his entire plan to any of his followers for fear that he might be betrayed. Nevertheless, Charleston officials eventually discovered the plot. At first, they were not sure who was leading the rebellion. But their investigations gradually brought them to Vesey. He was arrested and hanged, along with several of his co-conspirators.

Ten years after Vesey's hanging, a slave named Nat Turner led a revolt in Virginia that sent shock waves through the South. Turner was a respected preacher who claimed to have visions that whites and blacks would kill each other. One of these visions sparked his rebellion, which began on August 22, 1831. With a few followers, Turner attacked the homes of slave owners, killing their families and stealing their weapons. But Turner proved no match for the local militia, which killed some of his men in a bloody skirmish. Turner managed to escape and hide for weeks in the Dismal Swamp in North Carolina. Meanwhile, rumors swept the area that he was leading an enormous rebellion that threatened the lives of white citizens. Eventually, he was captured. Turner was rapidly brought before a judge, where he pleaded guilty and was hanged.

Many Southerners blamed the abolitionists, especially William Lloyd Garrison, for encouraging Nat Turner's rebellion. Garrison was personally opposed to violence but thought it might be necessary to overthrow slavery. In his newspaper, *The Liberator*, Garrison called Turner's revolt the first step on the road to freedom. "The first step of the earthquake, which is ultimately to shake down the fabric of oppression, leaving not one stone upon the other, has been made," Garrison wrote. "The first drops of blood, which are but the prelude to a deluge from the gathering clouds, have

Toussaint L'Ouverture was a former slave who led a revolution in Haiti. The uprising resulted in the abolition of slavery and establishment of a new government.

fallen."[3] The fears generated by Turner's rebellion gradually subsided, although slave codes were made harsher to prevent more revolts.

The *Amistad* incident occurred only eight years later. It looked to Southerners like another slave rebellion. Southern newspapers claimed that Cinqué and the other Africans were Spanish property, because they were slaves sold in Cuba. Southerners opposed any effort by the abolitionists to defend the Africans. They believed that the Africans should be returned to Cuba to stand trial for murder and rebellion.

Northern Responses to the *Amistad* Incident

As opposition in the South mounted, Dwight Janes continued his efforts to make sure that the Africans of the *Amistad* received a fair hearing. He wrote to Roger S. Baldwin, a prominent New Haven lawyer, hoping he would defend Cinqué and his followers. Janes also sent a letter to Joshua Leavitt of New York, an editor of *The Emancipator*, published by the Anti-Slavery Society. Janes asked Leavitt to find an interpreter for Cinqué so he could tell his side of the story. Early in September, Leavitt, along with Lewis Tappan and Simeon Jocelyn, a Congregational minister in New Haven, were appointed members of the *Amistad* Committee, made up of men from the area. It was charged with raising a legal defense fund for the Africans and ensuring that they were well cared for during the time they spent in the New Haven jail.

In New Haven, the adult Africans had been confined in three rooms, while the four children had a room to themselves. Cinqué was jailed by himself because he was considered more violent than the rest of the captives. Doctors who examined the prisoners found that they were suffering

Abolitionist Lewis Tappan, along with his brother Arthur, worked tirelessly to free the enslaved Africans of the *Amistad*.

from malnutrition. Because they were far from home and fearful of the future, many of them were too depressed to eat. Indeed, one had already died and others were sick.

Meanwhile, the *Amistad* Committee continued its efforts to free the Africans. They took out advertisements in newspapers, asking for contributions to the defense fund. Lewis Tappan wrote letters that were printed in the papers, trying to win sympathy for the prisoners. He also located an African in New York named John Ferry who might be able to communicate with the captives. Ferry talked to the Africans and seemed to understand some of their language. He believed that the children had been taken from Africa and sold as slaves. Meanwhile, newspaper accounts focused on Cinqué, who was rapidly becoming a celebrity. In local stores, people could buy wax figures and portraits of Cinqué and the other Africans. Five thousand people paid to see the prisoners in the New Haven jail. A play titled *"Amistad"* opened in New York to large audiences.[4]

Reactions to the *Amistad* captives in the North were mixed. While some newspapers agreed with the abolitionists that the Africans should be freed, others disagreed. Some believed that the blacks were better off in a state of slavery, that they were no better than apes and monkeys, and that the natural state of affairs between whites and blacks should be as master and slave. Northern journalists also criticized abolitionists like the Tappans for being publicity seekers.[5] As the *New York Morning Herald* put it: "The Abolitionists are determined to baffle those desirous of justice . . . All the whining . . . is . . . without the color of truth to support it."[6]

The newspapers reflected the attitudes of many Northerners toward slavery. They generally felt that this matter should be left to the South to handle. Northern industrialists who ran cotton mills recognized that they had a stake in slavery because several million slaves were necessary to pick cotton. Wage earners in the North also feared that a large population of free blacks might compete with them for jobs. A Frenchman named Alexis de Tocqueville, who traveled extensively in America during the 1830s, wrote about Northern racism in his book *Democracy in America*:

> Whoever has inhabited the United States must have perceived that in those parts of the Union in which the Negroes are no longer slaves they have in no wise drawn nearer to the whites . . . On the contrary, the prejudice of race appears to be stronger in the states that have abolished slavery than in those where it still exists. . . .[7]

Indeed, racism existed in many parts of the North. Free blacks had lost the right to vote in New York, Connecticut, New Jersey, and Pennsylvania. In Philadelphia, they were forced to attend segregated schools. In Canterbury, Connecticut, Prudence Crandall had tried to admit black children to her private school. White parents were so angry that they withdrew their children. When Crandall tried to start a school for blacks, townspeople lobbied the state legislature, which passed a law forbidding such a school to open. Crandall went to jail when she tried to defy the law. Later, when she wanted to reopen her school, the townspeople tried to burn down the building.

Much of the racism in the North was focused on the abolitionists. In 1834, for example, a mob stormed a meeting of the American Anti-Slavery Society and looted Lewis Tappan's home. A year later, in Boston, another mob

Prudence Crandall was arrested for trying to allow black children to attend her school.

left William Lloyd Garrison battered and bruised. But the strength of the abolitionists continued to increase during the 1830s as local antislavery societies spread across the Northern states. Now the abolitionists hoped that the *Amistad* case would focus national attention, once and for all, on the evil institution of slavery.

President Van Buren's Reaction

For its efforts to be successful, the *Amistad* Committee believed it was in a desperate race against time. The committee feared that President Martin Van Buren might act quickly to dispose of the case without a public trial. A Democrat, Van Buren held together a fragile coalition of Northerners and Southerners who had elected him in 1836. He planned to run for re-election in 1840 and he needed the support of the Southern slaveholders to ensure a victory. If the *Amistad* prisoners were freed as a result of a trial, it would definitely anger the South and cause him to lose the upcoming election.

Van Buren hoped he could solve this problem by simply honoring the treaty obligations that existed between Spain and the United States. According to Pinckney's Treaty of 1795, a Spanish ship and its cargo that had been forced into an American port by pirates should be returned to the control of Spain. On September 6, 1839, Spanish minister Angel Calderón de la Barca called on Van Buren to return the *Amistad* to Cuba under the terms of the treaty. Cinqué, according to the minister, had led a mutiny on a Spanish ship in Spanish waters. The United States, he said, had no authority over this matter. The minister wanted the Africans to stand trial in Cuba for mutiny and murder. Finally, the Spanish believed that the United States should take the same

President Van Buren supported sending the African captives back to Cuba to stand trial. He did not want to lose the support of the proslavery South.

position regarding these prisoners as it did with regard to its own slaves—namely, murder is not sanctioned in the name of achieving freedom. In other words, the *Amistad* Africans had no right to kill the crew members on the ship just to win their freedom.

President Van Buren wanted to go along with the Spanish minister's request. The United States district attorney in Connecticut, William S. Holabird, was immediately contacted by the Van Buren administration. Holabird would be involved in the case when it came up before the grand jury. He was warned by Secretary of State John Forsythe not to let the situation get "beyond the control of the Federal Executive."[8] Forsyth had already promised the Spanish minister that he would keep things under control. Clearly, the Van Buren administration was prepared to prevent the case from going too far. The administration had directed Holabird to get the case dismissed as soon as it went to court in Connecticut.

However, the president would soon discover that the *Amistad* incident was already taking on a life of its own. And there was little that he or his administration could do to stop it.

CHAPTER 5

Cinqué on Trial

The trials of Cinqué and the other *Amistad* defendants became the focus of people in the North and South. Newspapers ran accounts of the latest events that were read by Southern plantation owners and Northern abolitionists alike.

In September 1839, as the circuit court convened in Hartford, Connecticut, to hear the *Amistad* case, author William Cullen Bryant published a poem about Cinqué in the pages of *The Emancipator*:

Chained in a foreign land he stood,
A man of giant frame,
Amid the gathering multitude
That shrunk to hear his name—
All stern of look and strong of limb,
His dark eye on the ground—
And silently they gazed on him
As on a lion bound.
Vainly, but well, that chief had fought—
He was a captive now;

Yet pride, that fortune humbles not,
Was written on his brow.
The scars his dark broad bosom wore
Showed warrior true and brave;
A prince among his tribe before,
He could not be a slave.[1]

During the weeks leading up to the hearing, the abolitionists had tried to create the nineteenth-century equivalent of a media event by building as much support as possible for Cinqué and his fellow Africans. So far, this effort had been highly successful. The hotels in Hartford were crowded with people from as far away as Boston. They had come to see the prisoners as they were brought up from the New Haven jail. On the day the trial began, the courtroom was packed with onlookers and members of the press. Throughout the rest of the country, the abolitionists had also succeeded in focusing attention on the *Amistad* courtroom. From Cincinnati, Ohio, abolitionist James G. Birney wrote to Lewis Tappan, "The public sympathy here is decidedly in favor of the Africans at Hartford."[2] The *New London Gazette and General Advertiser* said that the slaves had been "feloniously [illegally] kidnapped and sold," adding, "was there not much . . . to justify them in acting as they did to regain that liberty and those rights of which they had been so wickedly deprived?"[3] Opinion in the South, however, was against the captives. A newspaper in Charleston referred to the *Amistad* Africans as a "piratical crew . . . their hands still reeking with the blood of murdered men. . . ."[4]

Poet and journalist William Cullen Bryant supported the cause of human rights and called for an end to slavery.

The Circuit Court Case

Presiding over the United States circuit court, Judge Smith Thompson listened as the lawyers for each side presented their arguments. The case before him involved charges of murder, mutiny, and piracy against Cinqué and the other prisoners. In addition, there were various claims against the *Amistad* and its cargo. Lieutenant Gedney of the USS *Washington* was claiming that he and his men were entitled to some reward, called salvage, for capturing the *Amistad* and the Africans on board. Captain Henry Green was also represented by a lawyer in court, who claimed that Green had detained Cinqué long enough for Gedney's men to capture him. In addition, Ruiz and Montes were represented by counsel, who demanded that the two Spaniards were entitled to have their slaves returned. Finally, United States Attorney William S. Holabird presented a claim from the Spanish government demanding that the *Amistad* and its captives be returned to Spain under the terms of Pinckney's Treaty.

On Thursday afternoon, September 19, attorney Roger Baldwin, representing the Africans, asked for a writ of habeas corpus for the three girls who had been aboard the *Amistad*. John Barber, who attended the trial, wrote that the "three African girls were brought into Court weeping, and evidently much terrified at the separation from their companions:—the eldest being about eleven years old."[5] Under a writ of habeas corpus, the girls were entitled to be freed if Baldwin could show that they were being held unlawfully because they had committed no crime. It was a bold strategy by the defense. Baldwin hoped to win sympathy from the judge by focusing the hearing on the defenseless little girls. He also

Justice Smith Thompson presided over the US circuit court when the *Amistad* case went to trial.

gambled that, if the girls were released under the writ of habeas corpus, it might mean that the judge would consider making the same decision for the other captives. This would be an admission that they were not slaves, but free human beings. As free human beings, they had had every right to rebel against Ruiz and Montes, who held them illegally. Therefore, they should be released from jail immediately.

Holabird, representing the government, strongly disagreed. He argued that the Africans were property that should be returned to the Spanish government. Nevertheless, he did state that, if the blacks had illegally been brought from Africa in violation of the international agreements regarding the slave trade, then they should be returned to their homeland. On Friday, Theodore Sedgwick—a member of the *Amistad* defense team—continued to present arguments in favor of the writ of habeas corpus. He produced evidence from interpreter John Ferry that the Africans had not been residents of Cuba but had been kidnapped from their homelands. However, Ralph Ingersoll, representing Ruiz and Montes, argued that there was no convincing evidence to prove that the Africans were not the legal property of his clients.

Despite strong opposition, the defense seemed to be gradually winning its case. This may have explained why Holabird finally stood up to make an unexpected announcement. "I stand here to contend that these blacks are free men—that they have been brought within the jurisdiction of the United States," he said, "and if found to be, as I suppose, native Africans, they may be sent to their native land."[6]

What the Judge Decided

After presenting their arguments, the lawyers for each side could now only sit and wait for Judge Thompson to deliver his verdict. As the judge began to speak, everyone in the courtroom listened closely. Thompson explained that the Africans could not stand trial in the United States for mutiny and murder, because their actions had taken place on board a Spanish ship in Spanish waters. Therefore, the United States courts had no jurisdiction over this matter. He denied the writ of habeas corpus. Instead, he said that the United States district court must decide whether the Africans were slaves and should be returned to Ruiz and Montes. He also said that the district court had to rule on the claims by Gedney and Green.

Thus, the abolitionists had rescued Cinqué and his companions from a murder charge. But they could still be returned to Cuba as slaves. There, they would probably stand trial and face execution.

Following the verdict, Judge Andrew Judson called the district court to order in Hartford, where the remaining issues would be heard. However, the case was postponed until November 19, to await more evidence that was important to the case. Judson was willing to grant bail for the Africans in the amount of their value as Cuban slaves. But the abolitionists would not admit that they were slaves, so Cinqué and his companions were returned to jail. Conditions improved for them, however. They were allowed to exercise outside, and the children were moved to a nearby private home.

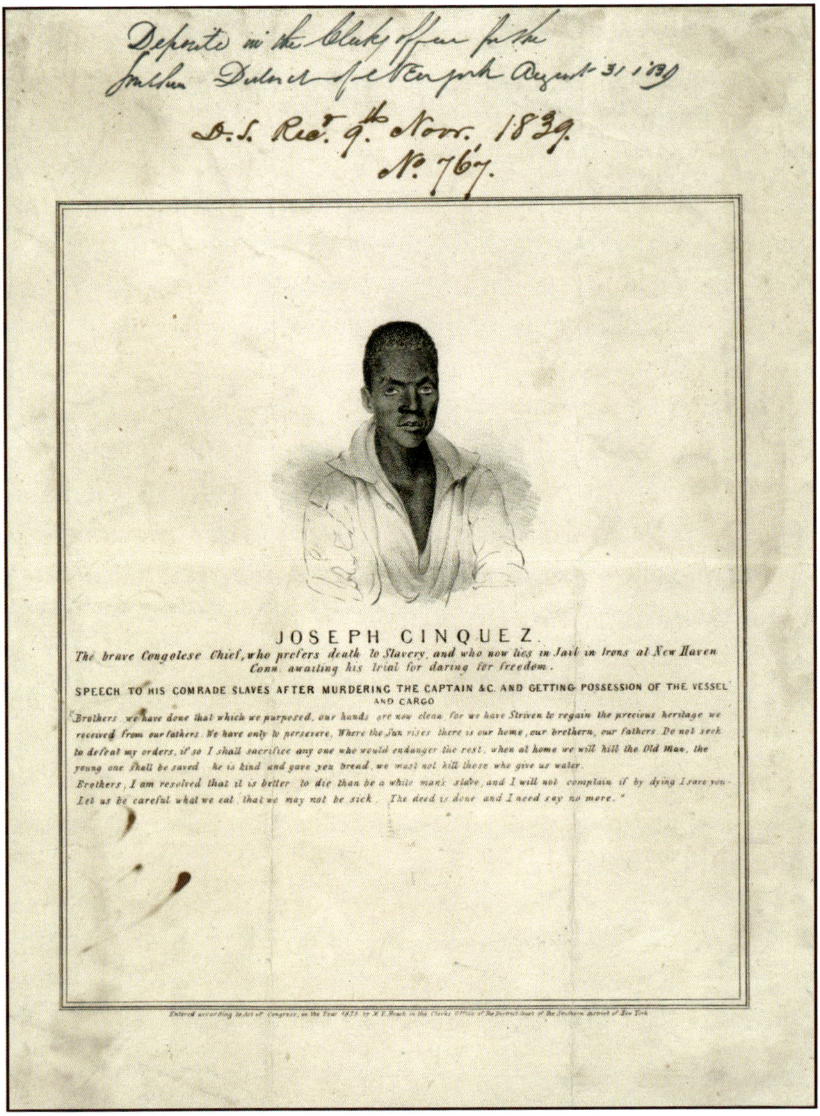

D. S. Recd. 9th Novr. 1839.
No. 767.

JOSEPH CINQUEZ.

The brave Congolese Chief, who prefers death to Slavery, and who now lies in Jail in Irons at New Haven Conn. awaiting his trial for daring for freedom.

SPEECH TO HIS COMRADE SLAVES AFTER MURDERING THE CAPTAIN &C. AND GETTING POSSESSION OF THE VESSEL AND CARGO

"Brothers we have done that which we purposed, our hands are now clean for we have Striven to regain the precious heritage we received from our fathers. We have only to persevere. Where the Sun rises there is our home, our brethern, our fathers. Do not seek to defeat my orders, if so I shall sacrifice any one who would endanger the rest. when at home we will kill the Old Man, the young one shall be saved he is kind and gave you bread, we must not kill those who give us water.

Brothers, I am resolved that it is better to die than be a white man's slave, and I will not complain if by dying I save you. Let us be careful what we eat that we may not be sick. The deed is done and I need say no more."

Many people felt sympathy for Cinqué and his fellow Africans. This portrait and account, which describe Cinque as a "brave" man who "prefers death to slavery," appeared in a New York newspaper in August 1839.

The Case Continues

While the district court was not in session, the *Amistad* case continued to be played out in the press. Ruiz and Montes told their story, claiming that they had not subjected the Africans to harsh treatment aboard ship. Meanwhile, the abolitionists searched for another interpreter to replace John Ferry. He had very little understanding of the language spoken by Cinqué and many of his companions. Eventually, an interpreter was found by Professor Josiah Gibbs of Yale University. James Covey was a linguist who tried to talk with Cinqué and believed he was speaking in Mende. Covey had been kidnapped from Mende country and forced aboard a slave ship headed for the Americas. Fortunately, the ship was stopped by a British patrol boat. Covey was freed, and eventually, he joined the British Navy. He was currently serving on a ship that was anchored in New York Harbor.

Covey found it easy to communicate with Cinqué, who described a long saga beginning with his capture in the African bush, his journey to the stifling barracoon of Pedro Blanco, and the terrible voyage across the Atlantic on the slave ship *Tecora*.

Cinqué then explained how he was smuggled into Cuba, where the Africans were eventually purchased by Ruiz and Montes. Finally, he described the revolt aboard the *Amistad*. Cinqué's story, along with those of other captives, was told through Covey to members of the press who had come to the New Haven jail.

Meanwhile, Lewis Tappan had decided on a bold move to throw Ruiz and Montes off balance. He persuaded Cinqué and several of the other Africans to file lawsuits charging the two Spaniards with assault, kidnapping, and wrongful

Attorney Roger Baldwin defended the rights of the *Amistad* captives.

imprisonment. Ruiz and Montes were arrested in New York and put into jail. Although Montes posted bail and left the country, Ruiz remained in confinement. But Tappan's strategy backfired. The Spanish government was angry that two of its citizens were being jailed. Many Americans also believed the abolitionists had gone too far. As the New York newspaper *Courier & Enquirer* put it, they were "making sport of the law and perverting the power of the courts of justice to . . . fanatical ends."[7]

The Case Goes to District Court

In November, Judge Judson continued the trial in district court. Roger Baldwin raised the issue of whether Connecticut had jurisdiction over the *Amistad* case, because Lieutenant Gedney had captured the ship and the Africans in New York. The abolitionists were trying to move the case to New York. They believed that there was strong racial prejudice in Connecticut, as shown by the Prudence Crandall case in 1831. In fact, Andrew Judson was the man who had led the fight to close down Crandall's school. Thus, the abolitionists feared he might not give their case a fair hearing.

Judson listened to Baldwin's argument as well as the salvage claims of Lieutenant Gedney and Henry Green. However, he did not make any final decisions. Instead, he postponed the trial until January in New Haven. Meanwhile, he heard testimony from Dr. Richard Madden, which was directly relevant to the case. Madden had lived in Cuba, serving on a commission that dealt with slave ships captured by British warships. These slavers had tried to bring their cargoes onto the island illegally. He was also responsible for the protection of the blacks who had been freed because they were brought to Cuba. Madden spoke to the captives in

New Haven. He became convinced that they were *bozales*—slaves who had been brought to Cuba illegally—not *ladinos*—residents of Cuba before the slave trade had become illegal. Many of the Africans were simply too young to have been longtime residents of the island. They also spoke no Spanish. Madden presented this testimony to Judge Judson.

Events in District Court

As the day of the district court hearing in New Haven came closer, the stakes in the case grew even bigger. The Spanish government, referring to the Africans as "assassins," demanded that they be returned to Cuba immediately.[8] The case had already gone on far too long for the administration of President Martin Van Buren. It was dividing opinions in the North and South, which might cost Van Buren his re-election. Attorney General Felix Grundy prepared a document stating that the Africans on the *Amistad* were slaves who belonged to Ruiz and Montes. The *Amistad*, Grundy said, was not involved in the illegal slave trade when the revolt occurred. The ship and its cargo should, therefore, be returned to Spanish control under the terms of Pinckney's Treaty.

Van Buren expected that the district court would agree with the attorney general and order the Africans to be sent back to Cuba. The administration told the Spanish that an American ship, the schooner USS *Grampus*, would be standing by in New Haven harbor to take the Africans immediately back to Havana. United States Attorney Holabird was also secretly instructed to transport the Africans to the *Grampus* before their lawyers had time to present an appeal. Thus, the administration was prepared to sidestep the legal system to

President Van Buren ordered the USS *Grampus* to be ready to return the Africans to Cuba quickly, before the defense lawyers could appeal the verdict.

achieve its goals and not let attorneys for the Africans appeal a decision that would send them back to Cuba as slaves.

The *Grampus*, under the command of Lieutenant John Paine, was anchored in New Haven harbor as the hearing resumed in Judge Judson's court. This time, Dwight Janes was called to the witness stand. He testified that Ruiz had admitted that the blacks had come from Africa. Testimony from James Covey confirmed that the Africans had been illegally transported to Cuba as slaves.

By far the most electrifying moment of the hearing occurred when the tall, muscular Cinqué strode slowly forward. Taking the oath, he gave his testimony. Cinqué told his story through the interpreter, James Covey. There had been rumors that Cinqué himself had been a slave trader, selling a man into slavery to pay off his debt. But he strongly denied this. John Barber, an eyewitness to the court proceedings, heard Cinqué's testimony:

> [He] described by actions, (which spoke louder than words,) the manner in which... [Ruiz] examined the Africans to ascertain if they were healthy and sound [examining their genital area]. He also put himself in the position in which they were forced to remain, when packed away on board the slaver.[9]

Afterward, two other Africans, Grabeau and Fuliwa, testified to the same facts. The prosecution tried to show that Cinqué had lied about being a slave trader. They also tried to prove that Dr. Madden's testimony was inaccurate. Holabird claimed that the blacks did not speak Spanish because they had continued to communicate in their native language long after arriving in Cuba. In addition, he said the *Amistad* had been authorized by the Cuban authorities to transport slaves from one port to another on the island. Meanwhile, Gedney's lawyer also presented his claim for a reward for capturing the ship and the Africans on board.

On January 13, 1840, Judge Judson finally handed down his decision. He ruled that the district court was authorized to hear the case because Gedney had captured the *Amistad* on the high seas, not in New York waters. Therefore, the case could come to trial in the state where he had landed the ship, Connecticut. Gedney was also entitled to salvage for his efforts—one third of the value of the vessel and its cargo. The *Amistad* and its cargo should then be returned to the Spanish government.

Finally, Judson answered the larger question: Were the Africans part of the ship's cargo? Were they property or were they free human beings? This was the decision that everyone in the courtroom had been waiting to hear. Judson ruled that the Africans had been brought into Cuba illegally. They were not slaves, but free men. Therefore, they had a right to rebel in order to regain their liberty. They could not be sent back to Cuba to stand trial for murder. They "shall not sigh for Africa in vain," he said. "Bloody as may be their hands, they shall yet embrace their kindred."[10] He ordered that they be handed over to President Van Buren and placed on an American ship that would take them back to West Africa.

Cinqué and his companions were finally going home.

CHAPTER 6

The Supreme Court Decides

The decision by the federal district court did not fully satisfy anyone. The abolitionists did not really get what they wanted. Southerners were furious that these Africans would be freed from slavery and allowed to return to their homes in Africa. Nor, as it turned out, was the administration of President Van Buren ready to accept the court's decision.

The Case Against Cinqué Continues

Around the time of the trial in district court, Cinqué, who was just beginning to learn the English language, wrote a short letter to abolitionist Lewis Tappan: "I will write you a few lines because I loves you very much," he began. "Cinque want you to go and See him. . . make this Menda men free to go to African. . .O please to let us go to the Africa. . ."[1]

Judge Judson's decision had apparently granted Cinqué his wish. He said they were "free" to go to Africa. But it was not quite the freedom Tappan and the other abolitionists had hoped for. Judson said he was carrying out a law passed by Congress more than twenty years earlier. It stated that it was unlawful to bring a black person from another country into the United States as a slave. The law also gave the president the authority to return that person home. But men who were truly free, Tappan knew, were not handed over to anyone—not even the president—to be taken anywhere. They were free to go wherever they wanted. Cinqué and his companions were not to be given the same rights as free whites in America—even though Judson had ruled that the blacks were free. The abolitionists had hoped that Cinqué and the other Africans would achieve equal footing with white Americans. This would be a first step to achieving equality for all blacks. However, Judson's decision had not given the *Amistad* captives this equality.

If this were not disappointing enough, at least as far as Tappan and the abolitionists were concerned, the administration of President Martin Van Buren then decided to challenge Judson's decision. United States District Attorney William S. Holabird was instructed to appeal the judge's ruling. Cinqué and the other Africans were not to be freed, after all.

Of course, Cinqué was extremely disappointed. What was this system of American justice that set a man free in one breath, only to keep him behind bars in the next? Holabird's appeal was heard at the next meeting of the circuit court, in April 1840, with Judge Judson and Judge Smith Thompson presiding. As everyone expected, they simply upheld the rulings made by their earlier courts.

This set up a final appeal by the government to the United States Supreme Court, the highest court in America. The Supreme Court justices agreed to hear the case in early 1841. It would prove to be a titanic struggle—with the

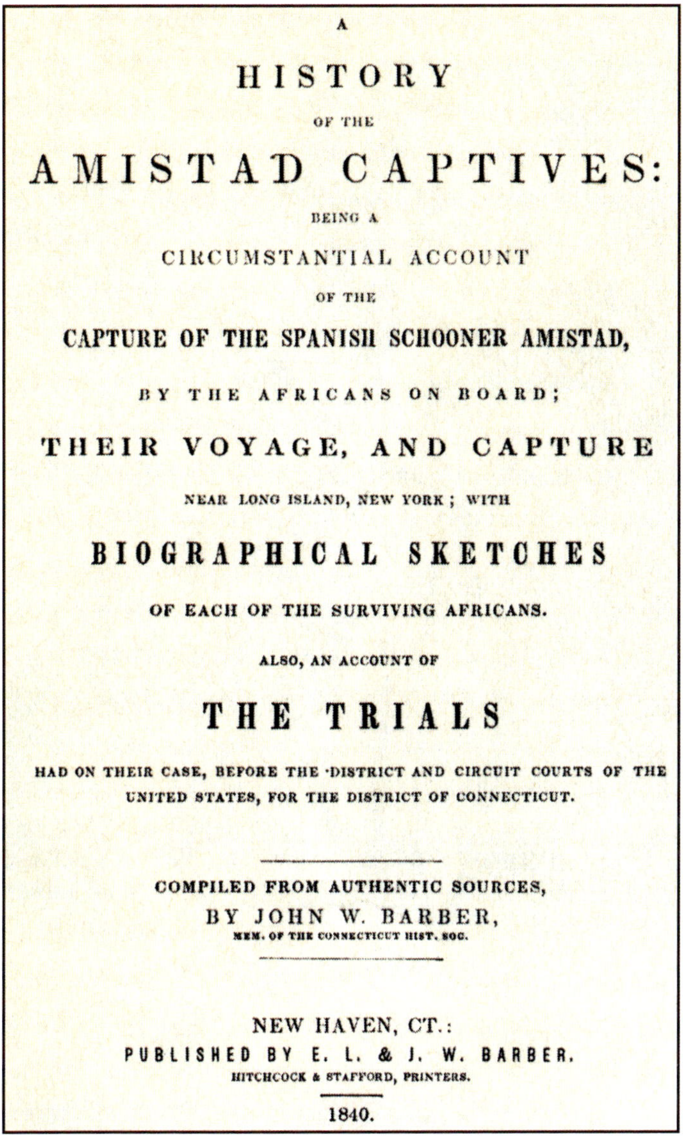

A

HISTORY

OF THE

AMISTAD CAPTIVES:

BEING A

CIRCUMSTANTIAL ACCOUNT

OF THE

CAPTURE OF THE SPANISH SCHOONER AMISTAD,

BY THE AFRICANS ON BOARD;

THEIR VOYAGE, AND CAPTURE

NEAR LONG ISLAND, NEW YORK; WITH

BIOGRAPHICAL SKETCHES

OF EACH OF THE SURVIVING AFRICANS.

ALSO, AN ACCOUNT OF

THE TRIALS

HAD ON THEIR CASE, BEFORE THE DISTRICT AND CIRCUIT COURTS OF THE UNITED STATES, FOR THE DISTRICT OF CONNECTICUT.

COMPILED FROM AUTHENTIC SOURCES,
BY JOHN W. BARBER,
MEM. OF THE CONNECTICUT HIST. SOC.

NEW HAVEN, CT.:
PUBLISHED BY E. L. & J. W. BARBER.
HITCHCOCK & STAFFORD, PRINTERS.

1840.

There was a great deal of public interest in the outcome of the *Amistad* case. John Barber of Connecticut, who witnessed the trial, wrote and published *A History of the Amistad Captives* in 1840.

freedom of Cinqué and the other *Amistad* captives hanging in the balance.

The Role of John Quincy Adams

Meanwhile, the African captives were moved out of New Haven to confinement in Westville, a few miles away. Students from Yale University visited regularly, instructing the Africans in Christianity, teaching them prayers, and helping them learn to read and write. Kali, a ten-year-old African boy who had been aboard the *Amistad*, seemed to learn English more rapidly than his companions. In 1841 he wrote a lengthy letter to former President John Quincy Adams, a strong opponent of slavery, who had been closely following the *Amistad* case:

> I want to write a letter to you because you love Mendi people and you talk to the grand court. We want to tell you one thing—Jose Ruiz say we born in Havana, he tell lie. . .We all born in Mendi—we no understand the Spanish language. . .We talk American language little, not very good; we write every day: we write plenty letters; we read most all time; we read all Matthew and Mark, and Luke, and John [books of the New Testament of the Bible], and plenty of little books. We love books very much. We want you to ask the court what we have done wrong. What for Americans keep us in prison.[2]

Lewis Tappan realized that the Africans' last chance to achieve freedom was the nine justices who sat on the United States Supreme Court. Five of them, including Chief

Justice Roger B. Taney of Maryland, were Southerners who might vote to send the Africans back to Cuba. Therefore, he reasoned, he needed someone with a national reputation and experience arguing cases in front of the nation's highest court to speak for the Africans. At first, Tappan approached Daniel Webster, a distinguished lawyer and United States senator. But he declined. Webster was busy and said he did not want to present a case before the Supreme Court. Tappan then decided to ask John Quincy Adams to represent the *Amistad* captives.

Adams was one of America's most experienced statesmen. When he was eleven years old, he had traveled to Europe as secretary to his father, John Adams, who had been sent to France to seek aid for the American Revolution. Later, John Quincy Adams would lead his own diplomatic missions as ambassador to Prussia and Russia. He also served as secretary of state during the administration of President James Monroe, becoming chief architect of the famous Monroe Doctrine. Elected president in 1824, Adams served only one term in the White House. He retired to Massachusetts, where he was elected a congressman in 1830.

As biographer Paul Nagel pointed out, Adams was never an abolitionist, but he was strongly opposed to slavery. In 1836 the House of Representatives had passed the gag rule, which prevented petitions opposed to slavery from being read on the House floor. Adams, who strongly supported free speech, did everything possible to overturn that rule and undermine the power of the slaveholders. "His adopted cause transformed him into a debater so impassioned, so mischievous, so stubborn, and so radical," Nagel wrote,

Former President John Quincy Adams spoke eloquently on behalf of the *Amistad* captives during the Supreme Court hearing.

"that his foes and even some friends wondered at times if he had lost his sanity."[3]

Adams was seventy-three years old when Tappan approached him. He had not argued a case before the Supreme Court in many years. No one knew his own shortcomings better than Adams, and at first, he declined the offer to handle the case. But Tappan insisted that he reconsider, and Adams finally agreed. He would join Roger Baldwin for the defense.

Meanwhile, Adams had successfully pushed a bill through Congress requiring the Van Buren administration to make public all correspondence relating to the *Amistad* case. As this information came out, Northern newspapers began printing articles claiming that Van Buren and Secretary of State John Forsyth seemed to have been supporting the position of the slave traders, Ruiz and Montes, as well as the government of Spain. When Ruiz and Montes were jailed, for example, Forsyth had told one of the government's legal officers to give them advice and aid that would help them win their freedom. In addition, the ship *Grampus* had been standing by during the district court trial to take the Africans back to Cuba, without waiting for their lawyers to file an appeal.

Adams would use this apparently improper interference by the Van Buren administration as his main line of argument during the Supreme Court trial. In addition, he met with Baldwin in New Haven and visited with Cinqué and his fellow Africans in jail. But even as he tried to prepare a strong case, Adams was forced to battle his own physical infirmities. "An inflammation in my left eye threatens me with complete disability to perform my final duty before the Supreme Court in the case of the *Amistad* captives," he wrote in his diary, "while the daily and hourly increasing weight of the pressure of preparation aggravates that disability."[4]

Adams was under no illusion as to the enormous task confronting him, although he may have been prone to overstate the role that he had been asked to play. He said:

> No one else will undertake it; no one but a spirit unconquerable by man, woman or fiend can undertake it but with the heart of martyrdom [dying for a cause]. The world, the flesh, and all the devils in hell are arrayed against any man who now in this North American Union shall dare to join the standard of Almighty God to put down the African slave-trade. . . .[5]

Arguments Before the Supreme Court

The case opened on February 22, 1841. US Attorney General Henry D. Gilpin presented the government's arguments as he paced back and forth before the justices. He argued that documents on the *Amistad* showed that the Africans were slaves owned by Ruiz and Montes, and should be returned to their owners under the terms of Pinckney's Treaty. Gilpin asked the justices to disregard testimony received from witnesses such as Dr. Madden.

Roger Baldwin then began his presentation. He stated that Cinqué and the others were not slaves, but free men unlawfully held by Ruiz and Montes. Once Baldwin was done, John Quincy Adams then rose to speak:

US Attorney Henry Gilpin tried to convince the court that the captive Africans were the property of Ruiz and Montes and therefore should be returned to their owners.

> The charge I make against the present Executive administration is that in all their proceedings relating to these unfortunate men, instead of that *Justice*, which they were bound not less than this honorable Court itself to observe, they have substituted *Sympathy!*—sympathy with one of the parties in this conflict of justice, and *Antipathy* [opposition] to the other. Sympathy with the white, antipathy to the black. . . .[6]

Adams then tried to demonstrate that, throughout the course of the *Amistad* case, the Van Buren administration had consistently given in to the demands of the Spanish government that the ship and the Africans be returned to their control. He cited a letter from Secretary of State John Forsyth to District Attorney Holabird, shortly after the ship was captured by Lieutenant Gedney. The letter stated that no action by the courts should place "the vessel, cargo, or slaves beyond the control of the Federal Executive."[7] Adams then cited evidence showing that President Martin Van Buren's administration intended to help Ruiz and Montes when they were in jail. The administration had also planned to smuggle the Africans onto the waiting ship *Grampus*—if the decision were made to return them to Cuba—without waiting to allow their lawyers the opportunity to make an appeal. The Spanish wanted public vengeance, Adams said. "What public vengeance? The vengeance of African slave-traders, despoiled of their prey and thirsting for blood! The vengeance of the barracoons! This 'public vengeance' is not satisfied."[8]

Adams completed his presentation after speaking to the Supreme Court justices for more than four hours. He was

Primary Source—John Quincy Adams Addresses the Supreme Court

MAY IT PLEASE YOUR HONORS—

. . . in a consideration of this case, I derive, in the distress I feel both for myself and my clients, consolation from two sources–first, that the rights of my clients to their lives and liberties have already been defended by my learned friend and colleague in so able and complete a manner as leaves me scarcely anything to say, and I feel that such full justice has been done to their interests, that any fault or imperfection of mine will merely be attributed to its true cause; and secondly, I derive consolation from the thought that this Court is a Court of JUSTICE. And in saying so very trivial a thing I should not on any other occasion, perhaps, be warranted in asking the Court to consider what justice is. Justice, as defined in the Institutes of Justinian, nearly 2000 years ago, and as it felt and understood by all who understand human relations and human rights, is—

"Constans et perpetua voluntas, jus suum cuique tribuendi."

"The constant and perpetual will to secure to every one HIS OWN right."

And in a Court of Justice, where there are two parties present, justice demands that the rights of each party should be allowed to himself, as well as that each party has a right, to be secured and protected by the Court.[9]

—John Quincy Adams argued his case before the United States Supreme Court in 1841.

supposed to continue speaking the next day. However, one of the justices—Philip P. Barbour—died unexpectedly that evening, and the case was not resumed until March 1. When the Court reconvened, Adams made another lengthy speech. He was followed by Attorney General Gilpin, who stated that President Van Buren had not interfered with the case and re-emphasized that the Africans should not be freed.

The Justices Decide

On March 9, the Court announced its decision. It was delivered by Justice Joseph Story, an opponent of slavery. The Africans were not slaves, Story said, and they should be freed. Furthermore, they had not been brought to America as slaves, but had been in control of the *Amistad* when it reached American waters. Therefore, they should not be handed over to the president. They should have the freedom to decide where they wanted to go. They were not pirates or robbers who had taken control of a ship. They had acted in self-defense to free themselves after being placed illegally in bondage.

When the decision had been handed down, the jailer and the United States marshal delivered the news to Cinqué and his companions in Westville. As one newspaper reported: "They were all assembled in one room, and on a signal from Cinque were seated. . . . The Marshal then showed them a newspaper and said 'here it is in the paper—read it.' Cinque beckoned to little Kali to read it aloud. . . ."[10]

There would be no more appeals. America's highest court had made a final ruling. This time, the Africans were really free.

Later, Cinqué would write a letter to John Quincy Adams:

Most Respected Sir,—the Mendi people give you thanks for all your kindness to them. They will never forget your defence of their rights before the great Court of Washington. They feel that they owe to you in a large measure, their delivery from the Spaniards, and from slavery or death. They will pray for you as long as you live, Mr. Adams. May God bless and reward you.[11]

CHAPTER 7

The Impact of the *Amistad*

After the decision by the Supreme Court, Cinqué and the other captives were finally able to walk out of jail. But where would they go next? The answer was a farm in Farmington, Connecticut. It was owned by A.F. Williams, who had played an important role in the abolition movement. His farm was an important destination for runaway slaves on the Underground Railroad. This network of abolitionists and free African Americans helped runaway slaves reach freedom in the North and in Canada. On Williams' farm, Cinqué and his friends spent the next few months improving their knowledge of Christianity and learning more English each day.

Because they were no longer in the custody of the federal government, Cinqué and his companions had to pay for their own food and clothing. They also wanted to raise the funds necessary to return home to Africa. While they were in Farmington, one of the Africans, named Foone, drowned in a canal, possibly committing suicide because he was so depressed at having been away from his homeland for such

Cinqué and the other freed Africans spent time on this farm owned by A.F. Williams in Farmington, Connecticut. Farmington was considered by many to be the "Grand Central Station" of the Underground Railroad.

a long time. The other Africans were eager to get back to Mende country as soon as possible.

In order to raise the funds the Africans needed, the *Amistad* Committee arranged for them to go on tour. Many Americans had followed the captives' story in the newspapers, and they were willing to pay to see Cinqué and the others in person. "Sixteen meetings were held," reported one newspaper. "The Mendeans read . . . spelt, answered questions . . . related their history in our tongue, sang native songs . . . and Cinque always made an address in his native language. . . . After he had concluded Kinna [one of the other Africans] interpreted what he said."[1]

The Africans also asked for assistance from the administration of the new president, John Tyler. "Now we want to go home, very much, very soon," Cinqué wrote to the president. "We want to see no more snow."[2] But Tyler was unwilling to help them unless a majority of legislators in Congress agreed to approve the expenditure. Congress turned it down. Nevertheless, enough funds were raised from the public tour, private donations, and money from a missionary society that wanted to establish a mission in Sierra Leone, Africa. On November 27, 1841, the thirty-five survivors of the original fifty-three Africans from the *Amistad* boarded the ship *Gentleman* to return to Africa. As they left from Boston, Cinqué, Kinna, and Kali wrote to John Quincy Adams: "We are about to go home to Africa. We go to Sierra Leone first, and then we reach Mendi very quick. When we get to Mendi we shall tell the people of your great kindness. . . . We will take the Bible with us. It has been a precious book, in prison, and we love to read it now we are free." They also sent a Bible to Adams as a gift for all he had done to help them.[3]

The newly free Africans appealed to President John Tyler for help in returning home, but he refused.

Once the *Gentleman* reached Africa, Cinqué headed for Mende country to find his family. But they had disappeared. He looked for them for many years. Although a few of the other Africans stayed at the Sierra Leone mission, most found new lives on their own. One of the little girls, Margru, returned to the United States and attended Oberlin College in Ohio—the first to offer coeducational classes and to admit African Americans. Later, she went back to Africa to teach at the mission. Cinqué died there in 1879. In the meantime, the mission had been moved to Sherbro Island, off the coast of Sierra Leone, where it was maintained by the American Missionary Association, which not only established international missions but led the struggle to eliminate the slave trade.

The Slave Trade Goes On

Following the decision in the *Amistad* case, the Atlantic slave trade continued. However, the British were making a better effort to stop it. An average of twenty British ships patrolled the waters off West Africa, and a large part of the coastline had been shut down to the slave trade. Indeed, British naval authorities estimated that, between 1839 and 1850, they had captured seven hundred slaving vessels and reduced the number of slaves leaving for America by almost two thirds.[4] However, the United States government still did not allow American ships to be stopped by Great Britain in its search for illegal slave traders. Consequently, Spanish or Portuguese slavers would hoist an American flag to prevent British officials from searching their ships or seizing their cargo.

Because American slave ships could not be captured by Great Britain, the United States government eventually

Primary Source—A Letter of Thanks

Mr. John Q. Adams
Dear Friend

We thank you very much because you make us free and because you love all Mendi people. They give you money for Mendi people and you say you will not take it, because you love Mendi people. We love you very much so we will pray for you when we rise up in the morning & when we lie down at night . . .Wicked people want to make us slaves but the great God who has made all things raise up friends for Mendi people he give us Mr. Adams that he may make me free . . . We write this to you because you plead with the Great Court to make us free and now we are free and joyful we thank the Great God. I hope God will bless you dear friend.[5]

—*An excerpt from a letter sent to John Quincy Adams by the freed* Amistad *rebels in 1841 following their return to Africa.*

added its own warships to the African patrol. Their purpose was to end the external slave trade to America, which had been declared illegal in 1808. However, slavers continued to bring in their cargo illegally because the slave trade was still very profitable. There were so few American warships patrolling the African coast that they caught only a handful of American slavers. In addition, some United States officials, who were from the South, were reluctant to prosecute other Southerners after they were caught.

Meanwhile, the slave ships kept transporting their cargo to the Americas, which were a ready market for slaves. Agricultural expansion in Cuba, Brazil, and the American South increased the demand for slaves. Ships were outfitted in ports such as New York, New Orleans, and Charleston for the slave trade. Finally, the British sent several warships to Brazil in the late 1840s, and they succeeded in capturing and burning some of the slave ships. This was the beginning of the end for the Brazilian slave trade.

Nevertheless, slaves continued to reach the United States, where they were sold at auctions in the South to work on the plantations. The *Amistad* incident had awakened many people to the evils of the slave trade. But it would take the efforts of the British Navy as well as the American Civil War to finally bring the slave trade to an end.

Abolitionists and Free-Soilers

The Supreme Court's decision in the *Amistad* case had very little impact on the institution of slavery. The Court ruled that the captives were not slaves, and therefore, they should not be returned to Cuba. However, the justices did nothing to overturn the principle that slaves in America were considered property. Indeed, the Court ordered that

After the *Amistad* trial, slavery continued to be an accepted practice in parts of the United States and in many other countries. At the same time, abolitionists like Wendell Phillips, shown here, became more vocal in speaking out against slavery.

Antonio—the slave who had belonged to the captain of the *Amistad*—should be returned to Cuba. He was later rescued by abolitionists and eventually went to live in Canada. Meanwhile, abolitionists continued their efforts to overturn the institution of slavery.

At first considered a fringe group of extremists, the abolitionists eventually gathered greater support in the North and helped form the Free-Soil Party, which nominated Martin Van Buren as its candidate for president in 1848. Van Buren had been forgiven for his role in the *Amistad* incident, and his fame as an ex-president seemed to make him a strong candidate. Free-Soilers wanted to stop the spread of slavery into new territories, fearing the political power of the South if the number of slave states increased. The United States had conquered a large western territory during the Mexican War (1846–1848) and this area became a battleground between proslavery and antislavery forces, especially when California petitioned for admission to the Union as a free state in 1850. Southerners wanted to extend slavery into these territories, while Northern political leaders were opposed. The two sides did not want to upset the balance of power in Congress, which was fairly evenly divided between proslavery and antislavery forces. Eventually, Congress agreed on a compromise. The Compromise of 1850 allowed California to enter the Union as a free state. At the same time, the settlers in the territories of New Mexico and Utah would vote on whether to allow slavery. This concept was called popular sovereignty.

For a time, a larger conflict between the North and the South over the issue of slavery seemed to have been avoided. But when the 1854 Kansas-Nebraska Act was passed, hostilities began again. The act set up the territories of Kansas and Nebraska, allowing settlers in each to vote on whether or not to allow slavery. Settlers there began battling violently over the issue. One of the antislavery men who participated in this conflict, John Brown, later led a raid on the United States arsenal at Harpers Ferry, Virginia, hoping to steal military weapons, arm the slaves, and unleash a massive slave revolt. Although he was later hanged, Brown became a martyr in the North. However, his raid made Southerners more determined than ever to hold on to their system of slavery.

In 1860 Abraham Lincoln was elected president and pledged to oppose the expansion of slavery westward. Southern states began to secede, or leave the Union. A bloody civil war would finally decide the future of slavery and the Union of the states.

In 1865, after the North won the Civil War that had raged since 1861, Congress began to pass a series of laws that outlawed slavery in the United States and gave African Americans the same rights as other citizens. Despite these gains, discrimination continued. In the Southern states, "Jim Crow," or segregation, laws were passed that prevented African Americans from attending the same schools as whites, or eating in the same restaurants. African Americans were also prevented from voting in elections. This discrimination would not begin to be eliminated until the civil rights movement that took place in the middle of the twentieth century.

Although great progress had finally been made, the Atlantic slave trade left behind a legacy of racism and cruelty. Even today, nearly two hundred years after the *Amistad* case, the slave trade continues to show its effects, both in the United States and in Africa.

A replica of the *Amistad* schooner enters the Havana, Cuba, harbor in 2010, on the tenth anniversary of its construction.

The *Amistad* Story Continues

The story of Cinqué and the *Amistad* was not forgotten. In 1997 producer Steven Spielberg made a historical film of the incident, starring actors Morgan Freeman, Nigel Hawthorne, Anthony Hopkins, Matthew McConaughey, and Djimon Hounsou. The film opened to strong reviews and grossed over $44 million.

In 2000 a replica of the *Amistad* was built in Mystic, Connecticut—not far from New London, where the original schooner was also constructed. The replica was built with a black hull and two masts, like the original sailing ship. Since its construction, the schooner has sailed across the Atlantic Ocean, through the Caribbean, and visited ports in the United States.

In 2010, the *Amistad* made an historic journey that took it from Virginia to Bermuda, the Dominican Republic, and the Bahamas, before arriving in Cuba. The ship first docked in the harbor of Matanzas before sailing eastward to Havana, arriving on March 25, 2010. This is the International Day of Remembrance of the Victims of Slavery and the Transatlantic Slave Trade.

"For us it's something indescribable," said Miguel Barnet, a Cuban historian. "This replica is very important because it recalls events that are dramatic and sad . . . history's longest holocaust."[6]

TIMELINE

1200s—Arab traders sell black slaves in Europe.

1400s—Portuguese explorers sail along the African coast and trade in slaves.

1510—Slaves begin arriving in Spanish America.

1619—First slaves arrive in Virginia.

1739—Stono Rebellion, led by a slave named Cato, is put down.

1740–1750—British merchants carry more than two hundred thousand slaves to the Americas.

1787—United States Constitutional Convention permits external slave trade until 1808.

1791—Toussaint L'Ouverture leads a slave revolt in Haiti.

1793—Eli Whitney invents the cotton gin.

1800—Slave revolt led by Gabriel Prosser is put down.

1821—American Colonization Society founds Liberia for freed slaves; Denmark Vesey leads an unsuccessful slave revolt in South Carolina.

1831—William Lloyd Garrison begins publishing *The Liberator*; Nat Turner is hanged after leading a failed slave revolt.

1833—Great Britain abolishes slavery in its colonies in the West Indies.

1839—Joseph Cinqué is captured in Sierra Leone and transported to Cuba as a slave; Cinqué leads a slave revolt aboard the *Amistad*; the *Amistad* is captured off Long Island by USS *Washington*; Cinqué and the other captives are jailed in New London, Connecticut; and circuit court hears *Amistad* case.

1840—United States district court rules that Cinqué and the other Africans are free and cannot be held as slaves; Government appeals to the United States Supreme Court.

1841—US Supreme Court hears the *Amistad* case; Court rules that Africans must be set free; Cinqué and other Africans return to Africa.

Timeline

1846–1848—Mexican War is fought; America gains western territories.

1850—Compromise of 1850 retains balance between proslavery and antislavery states.

1854—Proslavery and antislavery forces begin battling in the territories of Kansas and Nebraska.

1859—John Brown leads a failed raid on the arsenal at Harpers Ferry, Virginia; Brown is hanged.

1860—Abraham Lincoln is elected president; South Carolina secedes from the Union.

1861–1865—American Civil War is fought, ending in a Northern victory.

1865—Slaves are freed by the Thirteenth Amendment to the Constitution.

1879—Joseph Cinqué dies in Africa.

1997—Steven Spielberg produces the *Amistad* film

2000—Replica of the *Amistad* is built in Mystic, Connecticut.

2010—*Amistad* replica sails to Havana, Cuba.

CHAPTER NOTES

CHAPTER 1 Revolt at Sea!

1. Marcus Rediker, *The Amistad Rebellion: An Atlantic Odyssey of Slavery and Freedom* (New York: Penguin, 2013), 47.
2. Daniel Mannix, *Black Cargoes: A History of the Atlantic Slave Trade, 1518–1865* (New York: Viking, 1962), 231.
3. Thomas Howard, ed., *Black Voyage: Eyewitness Accounts of the Atlantic Slave Trade* (Boston: Little, Brown and Company, 1971), 3.
4. Olaudah Equiano, *The Life of Olaudah Equiano, or Gustavus Vassa the African* (Essex, England: Longman, 1988), 25.
5. Howard Jones, *Mutiny on the "Amistad": The Saga of a Slave Revolt and Its Impact on American Abolition, Law, and Diplomacy* (New York: Oxford, 1987), 23.
6. Doug Linder, "Newspaper Accounts of the Amistad Case," *Amistad Trial Page*, http://law2.umkc.edu/faculty/projects/ftrials/amistad/AMI_NEWS.HTM (accessed May 20, 2015).

CHAPTER 2 The Voyage Across the Atlantic

1. Aristotle, "Politics by Aristotle–Book 1," *Classical Wisdom Weekly*, accessed June 3, 2015, http://classicalwisdom.com/greek_books/politics-by-aristotle-book-i/2/.
2. Hugh Thomas, *The Slave Trade: The Story of the Atlantic Slave Trade, 1440–1870* (New York: Simon & Schuster, 1997), 41.
3. Olaudah Equiano, *The Life of Olaudah Equiano, or Gustavus Vassa the African* (Essex, England: Longman, 1988), 9–10.
4. Thomas, 69.
5. Ibid., 182.
6. Ibid., 185.
7. Ibid., 264, 370.
8. "Venture Smith relates the story of his kidnapping at the age of six (1798)," *NegroArtist.com*, accessed May 30, 2015, http://negroartist.com/writings/Venture%20Smith%20relates%20the%20story%20of%20his%20kidnapping%20at%20the%20age%20of%20six%20(1798).htm.
9. Thomas Howard, ed., *Black Voyage: Eyewitness Accounts of the Atlantic Slave Trade* (Boston: Little, Brown and Company, 1971), 120.
10. Ibid., 122–123.

11. Ibid., 80.
12. Steven Mintz, ed., "Excerpts from Slave Narratives – Chapter 1," accessed May 30, 2015, http://www.vgskole.net/prosjekt/slavrute/1.htm, from John Barbot, "A Description of the Coasts of North and South Guinea," in Thomas Astley and John Churchill, eds., *Collection of Voyages and Travels* (London, 1732).
13. Howard, 131.
14. Madeleine Burnside, *Spirits of the Passage: The Transatlantic Slave Trade in the Seventeenth Century* (New York: Simon and Schuster, 1997), 134.
15. Ibid., 125.
16. Thomas, 639.
17. William L. Andrews and Henry Louis Gates Jr., eds., "Interesting Narrative of the Life of Olaudah Equiano," *Slave Narratives* (New York: Penguin, 2000), 78–79.
18. John W. Blassingame, ed., *Slave Testimony: Two Centuries of Letters, Speeches, Interviews, and Autobiographies* (Baton Rouge: Louisiana State University Press, 1977), 242–243.

CHAPTER 3 The American Slave Trade

1. Damola Awoyokun, "Slavery and the Slave Trade: Felony, Reparations and Redress," *Nigerians in America*, March 17, 2007, http://www.nigeriansinamerica.com/slavery-and-slave-trade-felony-reparations-and-redress/.
2. Daniel Mannix, *Black Cargoes: A History of the Atlantic Slave Trade, 1518–1865* (New York: Viking, 1962), 194.
3. Warren S. Howard, *American Slavers and the Federal Law, 1837–1862* (Berkeley: University of California Press, 1963), 17–18.
4. Ibid., 111.
5. Edward Ball, *Slaves in the Family* (New York: Ballantine Books, 1999), 190.
6. Ibid., 89.
7. Peter Kolchin, *American Slavery, 1619–1877* (New York: Hill and Wang, 1993), 11.
8. Hugh Thomas, *The Slave Trade* (New York: Simon and Schuster, 1997), 271.
9. Mannix, 160.

10. Hunter D. Farish, ed., "Journal and Letters of Philip Vickers Fithian, 1773-1774, A Plantation Tutor of the Old Dominion" (Williamsburg: Colonial Williamsburg, Inc, 1965), 38–39.
11. Kolchin, 57.
12. John W. Blassingame, ed., *Slave Testimony: Two Centuries of Letters, Speeches, Interviews, and Autobiographies* (Baton Rouge: Louisiana State University Press, 1977), 219–220.
13. Mannix, 187.
14. Ball, 264.
15. "Results from the 1860 Census," *The Civil War Home Page*, 2009, http://www.civil-war.net/pages/1860_census.html.

CHAPTER 4 America and the *Amistad*

1. Louis Ruchames, ed., *The Abolitionists: A Collection of Their Writings* (New York: Putnam, 1963), 79–83.
2. Doreen Carvajal, "Slavery's Truths (and Tales) Come Flocking Home," *The New York Times*, March 28, 1999.
3. Truman Nelson, ed., *Documents of Upheaval: Selections from William Lloyd Garrison's "The Liberator," 1831–1865* (New York: Hill and Wang, 1966), 28.
4. Helen Kromer, *Amistad: The Slave Uprising Aboard the Spanish Schooner* (Cleveland: The Pilgrim Press, 1997), 39–40.
5. Howard Jones, *Mutiny on the Amistad* (New York: Oxford University Press, 1987), 48–49.
6. *New York Morning Herald*, September 13, 1939, from *"Amistad": A True Story of Freedom*, an exhibit at the Connecticut Historical Society, Hartford, Connecticut.
7. Alexis de Tocqueville, *Democracy in America* (New York: Knopf, 1994), 359.
8. Jones, 57.

CHAPTER 5 Cinqué on Trial

1. Howard Jones, *Mutiny on the Amistad* (New York: Oxford University Press, 1987), 66.
2. Dwight L. Dumond, ed., *Letters of James Gillespie Birney, 1831–1857* (New York: Appleton Century, 1938), vol. 1, 499.

3. *New London Gazette and Advertiser*, September 4, 1839, from *"Amistad": A True Story of Freedom*, an exhibit at the Connecticut Historical Society, Hartford, Connecticut.
4. *The Southern Patriot*, Charleston, South Carolina, September 10, 1839, from *"Amistad: A True Story of Freedom"*.
5. John Barber, *A History of the Amistad Captives* (New York: Arno Press, 1969), 16.
6. Jones, 76.
7. Clifton Johnson, *The Amistad Case and Its Consequences in U.S. History* (New Orleans: The Amistad Research Center, 1999), 5.
8. Jones, 111–112.
9. Barber, 20–21.
10. Johnson, 9.

CHAPTER 6 The Supreme Court Decides

1. John W. Blassingame, ed., *Slave Testimony: Two Centuries of Letters, Speeches, Interviews, and Autobiographies* (Baton Rouge: Louisiana State University, 1977), 33.
2. Ibid.
3. Paul C. Nagel, *John Quincy Adams: A Public Life, a Private Life* (New York: Knopf, 1997), 356.
4. Allan Nevins, ed., *The Diary of John Quincy Adams, 1794–1845* (New York: Scribner's, 1951), 516.
5. Ibid., 519.
6. John Quincy Adams, *Argument in the Case of United States vs. Cinque* (New York: Arno Press, 1969), 6.
7. Adams, 12.
8. Ibid., 38.
9. "JQA Adams Before the Supreme Court," *History Central*, accessed May 30, 2015, http://www.historycentral.com/amistad/amistad.html.
10. *The Philanthropist*, Cincinnati, Ohio (March 3, 1841).
11. Blassingame, 42–43.

CHAPTER 7 The Impact of the *Amistad*

1. *The Philanthropist*, Cincinnati, Ohio (December 29, 1841).

2. John W. Blassingame, ed., *Slave Testimony: Two Centuries of Letters, Speeches, Interviews, and Autobiographies* (Baton Rouge: Louisiana State University Press, 1977), 42.
3. Ibid., 43.
4. Daniel Mannix, *Black Cargoes: A History of the Atlantic Slave Trade, 1518–1865* (New York: Viking Press, 1962), 264.
5. Meghan Keneally, "Thank You Letter From Amistad Rebellion Slaves to John Quincy Adams Released," *ABC News*, July 7, 2014, http://abcnews.go.com/US/letter-amistad-rebellion-slaves-john-quincy-adams-released/story?id=24458410.
6. Will Weissbert, "Replica of 1839 Slave Ship Amistad, originally from Cuba and Rebuilt in US, Docks in Havana," *Chicago Tribune*, March 29, 2010, http://www.chicagotribune.com/ct-travel-amistad-replica-in-cuba-story.html.

GLOSSARY

abolitionists—Reformers who wanted to bring an end to slavery and the slave trade.

barracoon—A slave barracks for holding captured Africans.

black gold—A popular term to describe black slaves.

bozales—Slaves brought to Cuba illegally.

conquistadors—Spanish explorers who conquered the New World.

habeas corpus—The right of a person to be brought before a court and charged with a crime instead of being held in prison without charge.

Jim Crow laws—Laws that forced African Americans to use segregated facilities, like hotels and restaurants, and to live in segregated neighborhoods.

Ladinos—Slaves living in Cuba before the slave trade was outlawed.

Middle Passage—The trip by slave ships across the Atlantic Ocean from Africa to America.

racism—Prejudice against people of different ethnicities.

salvage—Compensation or reward for the rescue of a ship and/or its cargo.

segregated schools—Separate schools for white children and children of other ethnicities.

slaver—A ship used to transport slaves; a person involved in the slave trade.

triangular trade—The trade between North America, Africa, and the Caribbean involving sugar, slaves, and rum.

Underground Railroad—A network of individuals who helped escaping slaves reach freedom.

FURTHER READING

Books

Elish, Dan. *John Quincy Adams*. New York: Benchmark, 2011.

Grayson, Robert. *The Amistad*. Edina, Minn.:ABDO, 2011.

Greenhaven Press Editor. *Slavery through the Ages*. San Diego: Greenhaven Press, 2014.

Marcovitz, Hal. *The History of Slavery*. San Diego: ReferencePoint, 2014.

Marrin, Albert. *A Volcano Beneath the Snow: John Brown's War Against Slavery*. New York: Knopf, 2014.

Websites

National Archives

www.archives.gov/education/lessons/amistad

Includes primary source documents related to the Amistad.

History Channel

www.history.com/topics/amistad-case

Provides videos, articles and pictures of the Amistad *case.*

National Portrait Gallery

www.npg.si.edu/col/amistad

Includes background information as well as pictures of participants in the Amistad case.

INDEX